HOW TO ANALYZE PEOPLE

GUIDE TO SPEED READING PEOPLE TO RECOGNIZE PROHIBITED MANIPULATIONS AND DARK PSYCHOLOGY AT FIRST SIGHT, AND TO PROTECT YOURSELF FROM MENTAL HACKING.

John Austin

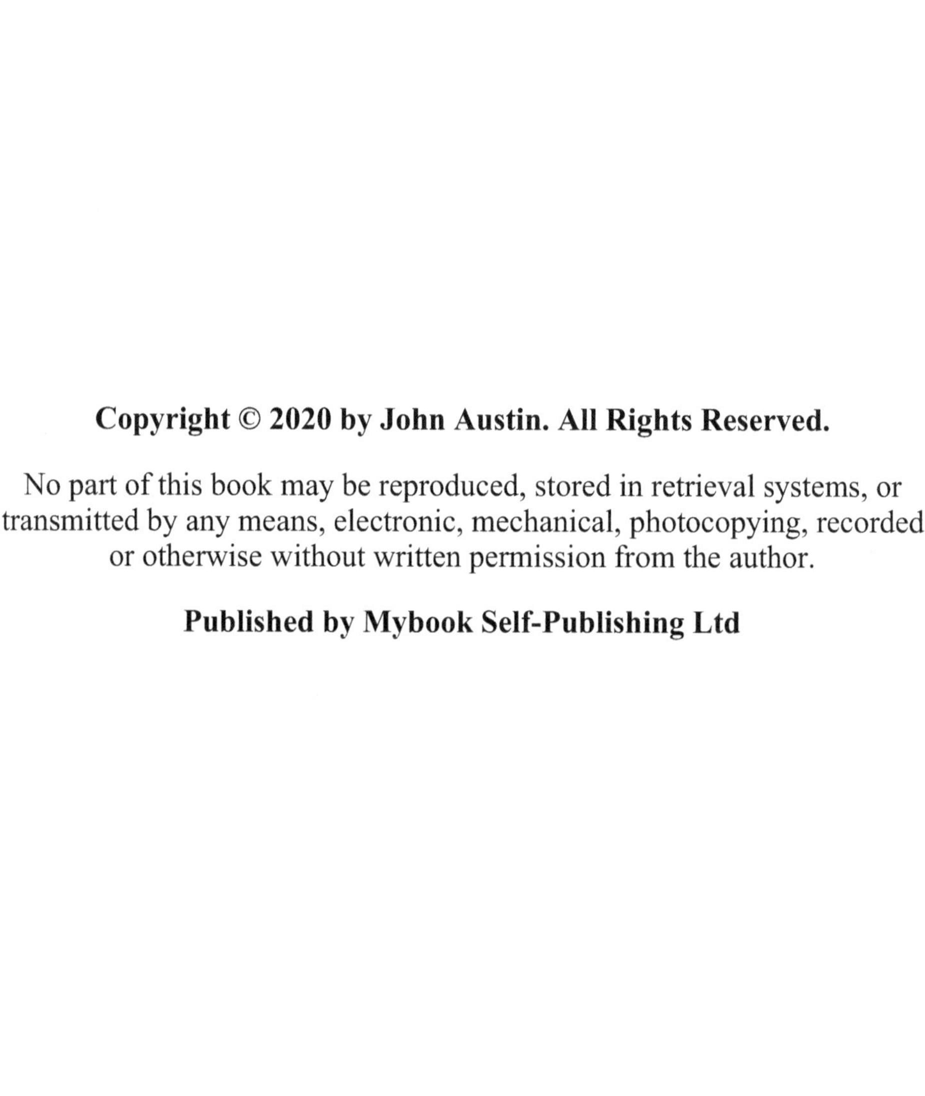

Table of Contents

Introduction

One may conclude that understanding body language is a useless skill because we have the gift of verbal communication. While the art of linguistics is certainly necessary to communication, oftentimes, words only tell a small truth. People who lack the proper understanding of the connection between the body and mind will miss these slight signals. For example, the slight curve of the lips combined with a forward lean speaks attraction even if the words being spoken reveal the opposite. Imagine having the ability to detect when someone was lying by observing a simple eye movement.

There is a dynamic structure of the brain called the limbic system that is responsible for controlling how our emotions translate throughout our bodies. The limbic system controls our inner qualities such as the ability to nurture, express empathy, and even react to love. When your face suddenly blushes because you see your crush, that is your brain responding to the emotion of attraction. Without the limbic system, it would be increasingly difficult to be able to openly express our emotions through physical contact.

Animals Use Body Language to Communicate

Dogs are classic examples of animals who rely heavily on body movements to express themselves. Since they cannot verbalize their emotions to humans, they use their ears, paws, and even their tails to signal important symbols. Universally, a dog's tail wagging has been accepted as a dog showing his friendliness. However, not every wag is welcoming. A stiff, low wagging tail can indicate feelings of uneasiness. A straight, pointed wag is a sign of impending attack. Someone who generalizes all tail wagging as welcoming may encounter an unpleasant situation without the proper knowledge. Dog trainers initially begin their training with body movements to assign meanings to commands.

The same mentality rings true with humans. Many people may say one thing to appease the person they are around, yet their true intentions are masked. By understanding the psychology behind body language, you will be able to actually read people without them even knowing it. This ability comes in handy for the following situations:

- Raising a child

- Understanding your mate's true feelings

- Detecting lies or deception

- Spotting insecurity

- Emergency situations

Once mastered, you will be able to further develop your analytical skills and hone in on your ability to decode human behavior.

When raising young children, the ability to effectively communicate needs doesn't become apparent until around 15 months. Babies and toddlers rely heavily on certain nonverbal cues when communicating their needs. For example, children who experience inner conflict and lack the ability to express themselves verbally may bite their parents or peers as a means to seek attention. This oral fixation is their way of getting their needs met. It is important for parents to understand the subtle movements of others in order to accurately meet the needs of their children.

Chapter 1 Speed reading people

As explored, there are many stimuli that trigger human responses and lead to decision-making, and researchers have developed extensive methods to measure these outcomes, whether using biometrics, surveys, or focus groups. However, these research methods may not be at your disposal on a daily basis. Below are methods techniques you can use in everyday interactions to analyze cognitive and behavioral processes of individuals around you.

Observe Body Language

Research found that body language accounts for 55% of how we communicate, while words only account for 7%. The tone of voice represents the rest. People can tend to be over-analytical when reading human behavior and it may seem counterintuitive, but in order to be objective in analyzing people, observe naturally and try not to over-analyze.

Appearance

One of the first things that speak the loudest is the appearance of an individual. Take notice of a person's dressing. Is he or she dressed sharply in a suit, traditional clothing, or casual style? Does he or she look particularly conscious about the choice of clothing or hairstyle? The way a person dresses can determine his or her level of self-esteem.

Posture

When reading people's posture, observe if they hold their head high or slouch. Do they walk indecisively or walk with a confident chest? How do they esteem themselves? Posture also reveals confidence levels or a person's physical pain points.

Movements

People generally lean towards things they like, and away from things they do not. Crossed arms and legs suggest self-protection, anger, or defensiveness. When people cross their legs, their toes point to the person they are most comfortable with, or away from those they are not. When hands are placed in pockets, laps, or behind the back, it is an indication that the person is hiding something. Nervousness can also be revealed through lip-biting or cuticle-picking. Some people do that to soothe themselves under pressure or in awkward situations.

Facial Expressions

Aforementioned, emotions may not be visible unless expressed. Frown lines indicate over-thinking or worry, while crow's feet evidence joyfulness. Tension, anger, or bitterness can be seen on pursed lips or clenched jaws. Facial expressions can be one of the most evident ways to read human behavior towards specific things, places, or people.

Chapter 2 How to analyze people effectively and efficiently

So, you want to learn how to analyze people effectively and efficiently. Well, you came to the right place! I will teach you everything you need to know about reading others. I will even teach you how to understand yourself. We need to talk about a few things before we get into the meat of the matter, however.

There are so many different methods to analyze others, and it can be hard to pick it all apart. Where did this practice come from? Why is it important to understand how to analyze others?

As it turns out, the art of analyzing others has existed since—well, we had the intelligence to do it. Human beings are, by nature, herd animals. We are highly in tune with others, and our lives are driven by societal expectations. It can be easy to get caught up in our instincts, though, and to forget that we need to tackle things logistically. This is where learning how to actively analyze others comes in.

Studies consistently show that we are attracted to confidence and leadership. We like to take the burdens of everyday life and put them on other people's shoulders. Part of this is allowing ourselves to be far too trusting in situations where we would benefit from awareness surrounding red flags. Unfortunately, people are not always genuine; they can be terrible–evil, even. This is a world where we need to be on high alert. While analyzing people will help you in many aspects, such as work and in leadership roles, it can also help keep you safe.

Being situationally aware is simply not in practice anymore. People are constantly unaware of their surroundings and putting themselves in harm's way as a result.

So, as you can see, there are many reasons to unravel the techniques of analyzation. Scanning people for warning signs or just for information about them puts you ahead of the pack. There is nothing more beneficial to your life, your relationships, and your protection. Spot narcissists before they have a chance to victimize you. Understand your boss's motives and learn how to nail down what they want from you, without even hearing them say it.

Here are some jobs which actively employ analyzing others:

- Politicians

- Lawyers

- Criminal investigators

- Military officials

- Psych professionals

- Forensic experts

As you can see, it truly is a universal tool. Many different people have to analyze others daily in their day-to-day lives.

I hope that these are the skills you want to learn. They are invaluable, and it is my pleasure to help you improve your life, one impression at a time.

There are, of course, incredible benefits to consuming the knowledge I am offering to you today. First off, you will find that you can communicate your needs to other people far more effectively. Being able to tell how they are reacting and changing your approach accordingly is more than helpful. Communication is the most important skill that we can hone, quite frankly. It helps ease tension, earn the confidence of others, and put us in a positive light. Emotional intelligence goes hand in hand with communication as well.

This is another skill that will be furthered when paired with the power to analyze others. Your emotional intelligence greatly relies on your ability to understand others. The goal is always to meet people where they are: understanding what they need and being able to tell how they need to be handled. Whether you lead a team, need to help your children through their struggles, or are feeling the tension in your love life, I am here to help.

Strong relationships are the glue of society and, more importantly, of families. We need to know how to handle our spouses, children, and anybody else directly related to us.

Strained relationships lead to strained relations, and none of us want to be caught up in a family feud. Learning how people tick and how to handle tough situations is the key. You will also learn how to watch for red flags with your children. Knowing how to read their body language and pick up on their verbal cues do wonders for seeing warning signs well in advance.

If you are a parent, this will be a key book in taking your parenting to the next level.

As for another skill, leadership, you will soon be at the front of the crowd. You will find that people not only listen to you but that they actively want to listen to you. Becoming a strong leader means being able to tell who a person is just by carefully observing them. True leaders understand the absolute power that body language holds. After all, it is the oldest form of communication of them all.

Many leaders in the business world, as well as in other areas, actively take lessons and classes on analyzing others. This is a skill which can be applied in almost every situation you can think of. It builds your confidence knowing that when you take the lead, others follow suit.

I am pretty sure you are beginning to get the idea of what analyzing others can do for you. The benefits are boundless, and there are new ones at every corner. You cannot imagine how much life will change!

I would like to get you started with a few rules. As you can imagine, there is a baseline to start when it comes to analyzing others. You can remember some steps to help you begin which are not hard and fast but excellent for helping you to understand the process. Practice makes perfect, so make sure you pay close attention to this list.

These rules are as follows:

1. Understand What Their Baseline Is: Everybody is just a tad bit different from the rest. It is almost like how parents can tell their twins apart, but nobody else can. Learning how to analyze others means you can tell them apart on a much different level. Understand that you can only tell their "baseline" after knowing them for a while.

You can watch for signs that they are nervous. Perhaps ask probing questions you know will elicit the emotion you want to pin down. If they tend to become physical restless under duress, you know what sort of body language to watch for.

This is the first rule for many reasons. Most importantly, it reminds us that we need to see the whole person. Cold reading is great. We will go over it later in detail, but true analyzation takes time and consideration.

2. Notice the Changes: Take into account the entire picture of the person. This builds off of the first rule.

Understand that any gesture can mean something, but you need to put several clues together to really solve the mystery that is a person.

This will also build off of noticing what signs of nervousness you may be looking for. We are using nervousness for these examples, but it goes for any emotion. Anger, unease, discomfort–they are all negative emotions you can begin to pinpoint.

3. Watch For Warning Signs. When certain behaviors are brought into the light and therefore meaning in your eyes, you can start to piece it together. If you have noticed that they shift their eyes around when nervous, and their eyes tighten up when they are angry, you will know when you are treading on dangerous territory.

There are several different clusters of behaviors that can be seen across the board. As mentioned, humans are pack animals in nature. This means that we have learned how to communicate with each other whether we like it or not. Certain tip-offs are pretty well-known. However, a lot more will be missed to the untrained eye. That is why you are reading this!

4. Compare Behavior Changes: The next rule in this line-up is to always make sure you watch how they behave with others as well. It is a popular belief that you do not watch the person who is speaking–you

watch the reaction of the person you want to impress. Making sure you are taking note of your boss's body language while listening to co-workers, for example.

Notice the changes between them talking to you and them talking to others. This will help cue you into their true emotions about you as well as how they feel about others. Are their arms crossing when they talk to their friends? Is their body still turned towards you even while engaged in conversation elsewhere?

5. Watch Yourself. One of the most powerful things you can do is be aware of your body language. We do not just need to understand others but also ourselves. We influence others with our facial expressions without even knowing what it looks like. That is not what you want to be doing. To control a situation or a conversation, or even influence it, you need to practice expressions.

The best way to do this is to do it in the mirror. Again, this will be gone over in-depth later on. I guess I just keep giving you small teasers!

6. Listen To Others Talk. Identify the strongest person in the room. You will notice them right away, most likely. Sometimes, however, it takes a little time. Look for open body language being used purposefully but elegantly. A big smile, a voice that commands attention and self-confidence are all ways of saying "I

am the boss in this situation." They do not need the approval of others and they often hold the most sway in the situation.

Same idea as watching the boss when others are talking. Even if somebody is technically the boss, that does not mean they are completely in control. A confident, strong person will make an impression and quickly become somebody whose opinion the "head honcho" deeply trusts. Knowing which strings to pull will push you further and further toward getting what you want out of a situation.

7. Watch Them Move. Looking at body language while they talk to you, especially sitting or standing still, is one thing. You also need to watch their general state of being while moving around. You can tell quite a bit about a person just by the way they walk and how they move. Confident people tend to stand tall, with their shoulders back and chest pushed a little out. They walk with purpose, as though they always have somewhere important to be.

On the other hand, somebody who is unsure of themselves embodies the exact opposite traits. They try to make themselves look small, perhaps hunching over a little, keeping their head low.

8. Listen For Speech Patterns. Another rule is to listen closely to how they talk and what they are saying, both

about the topic at hand and about themselves. How a person speaks tells you so much about them, both literally and figuratively! When you can identify how they speak when they are being truthful and genuine, you can figure out when they are being the opposite.

There are several different ways to go about this. However, looking for "action words" is one of the best. A lot of ex-agents talk about how looking for these words, especially strong verbs; it helps you figure out how their brain works. These words do not just convey their thoughts but they convey the patterns of their thoughts as well.

9. Key Into Their Personality. The last rule is to always put all of this information together. You cannot use one of these rules without following up with the others. These are the cardinal tenets off of which all analyzation of others is built. Once you put together their verbal communication, their body language, and understand them as a whole, you have won half the battle.

It is especially important in the art of analyzing people that you follow this rule. Humans are, by nature, endlessly complex. We cannot be understood by just one piece of information or even a few pieces. Think of it like putting together a puzzle. In the beginning, you have no idea what the result will be. Once you begin to put some of the pieces together, you begin to understand the whole picture. You can even fill in some of the missing pictures once you have enough of those pieces.

So, as you can see, you eventually will build your skillset until you can fill in more information with only some of the pieces. But you still need those pieces.

These rules should be followed at all times. Keep them in mind whenever you go about trying to figure anybody out. They are key in your journey through the art of analyzation!

The last thoughts in this chapter that I will leave you with are the differences between intuition and paranoia. It can be easy to misunderstand which is which, especially when dealing with potentially dangerous situations. However, mixing them up due to inexperience or simply not knowing the difference can be far more troublesome. Paranoia at its most extreme form is a symptom of many mental illnesses. None of us are immune to falling into the trap of poor thought patterns which encourage paranoia to take hold. It is a sinister feeling that we all need to keep at bay.

Intuition is rooted almost solely in logic. It is the idea that you have cultivated an array of experiences in your life that you can compare to the situation at hand. It is a result of insight as well as the ability to properly analyze others. You will feel calm, stable, and rational when your intuition is kicking in. It does not feel like it is "forced" upon you in the same way that fear does.

You have control over intuition and can reason your way through even the negative thoughts that come your way.

You can ascribe the following words to intuition:

- Collected

- In control

- Gentle

- Freeing

- Enlightening

As you can see, intuition is a highly positive emotion you should nurture. Always listen to that inner voice which nudges you towards good ideas. With a little bit of attention, you can quickly decide whether it is intuition you are feeling or simply anxiety and fear.

Speaking of which, let us talk a little bit about fear now. This is a strong emotion that overwhelms you. Fear eats away and pushes you towards rash behavior. You know fear well—we all do. This is an emotion we have all felt, probably many times over our lifespans. You cannot count how many times it has crept into your brain. It is not just an emotion, however.

It is something far more powerful. Fear can actively change the way you think and your ability to respond to situations. The part of the brain which controls it, the amygdala, shows signs of hyperactivity when you feel fear, and your frontal lobe's activity is stunted. These two regions are responsible for your reactions, your impulses, and your behavior.

Those are not the parts of yourself that you want to fall short on!

If it is fear you are feeling, the following words may suit it:

- Apprehensive

- Impulsive

- Irrational

- Cagey

- Insecure

Once you begin to tell the difference, you begin to take control back. Managing your negative emotions properly is one of the best steps in building your self-control. It also allows you to stay focused on situations even if they feel dangerous in any way. Remember, something does not have to be physically threatening to feel dangerous. It can just be feeling like you are about to be fired. It can strike when you feel like your partner is falling out of love.

These are the situations where it becomes important to tell them apart. Your partner is most likely not falling out of love with you. That is most likely your fear or anxiety speaking. However, when you can tell it apart from intuition, you will know whether these thoughts hold any validity.

Chapter 3 Perception

Perception refers to the set of unconscious processes a person goes through to make sense of the sensations and stimuli the individual encounters. Your perception is based on your interpretation of the various sensations and the impressions you get from the stimuli that you get from the world around you. Perception is what helps you navigate the world because it guides your decision-making process, from what to eat for breakfast, the clothes to wear, the relationship to be in and the reaction you give to something dangerous that is coming your way.

If you close your eyes and try to remember the details in the room you are in, do you remember the color of the walls? Do you recall the location of the furniture there? Do you remember the angle that the shadows make? Whatever you can or cannot remember is guided by your perception. Your brain cannot remember everything it encounters; you will only take note of some things, guided by your perception.

The difference in perception of one person from another is best illustrated by an optical illusion where if you and your friend look at the illusion, you are likely to note one thing, while your friend will note something entirely different. The difference is brought by the variation in the processes that the brain goes through to create your reaction or perception of stimuli. These processes are selection, organization, and interpretation.

This is the last stage of perception; it is the stage in which a person subjectively considers and understand stimuli. This is the stage in which we attach meaning to what we see.

Interpretation is influenced by experiences, beliefs, cultural values, self-concept, needs, expectations, involvement, and other individual influences. Experience plays a primary role in understanding behavior. For example, a person who has gone through physical abuse might interpret a person raising his hand towards them as someone who wants to hit him or her. On the other hand, a person with a sports background could interpret the same gesture as someone leaning in for a high-five, and he will raise his hand too.

Culture provides a structure, rules, expectations, and guidelines to govern behavior. Based on these variations, you will note that people understand, interpret and respond to behavior in different ways. For example, Americans mothers are known for celebrating their children's successes, however slight. Chinese mothers are known for their focus on discipline. Based on this difference, what would appear to the Chinese mother as a lack of discipline, an American mother might interpret as basic childhood curiosity and exploration.

Self-concept is also a crucial influence on the viewpoint a person has. Self-concept refers to the pool of thoughts and beliefs a person has about himself in regard to his racial identity, sexuality, intelligence, and others. If you believe that you are an attractive person, you will likely interpret stares you get from other people as admiration for your beauty. However, if you think you are unattractive, you will consider the stares to be negative judgment.

Desire and expectations can determine how you interpret stimuli. An individual's desire to avoid the negative stimuli causes him or her to interpret stimuli in a particular way.

The role of schemata

Interpretation of behavior is a conscious and deliberate event in which a person attaches meaning to the experiences he has had using mental structures called schemata. Schemata can be likened to databases that store the information that you use when you interpret new experiences. All of us have schemata, and they are different because of the variations in the experiences we have gone through over time. The bits of information from each event combines with bits from other incidents resulting in a complex web of information.

For example, you have an overall schema in regard to how you interpret education due to the experiences you have had in school when interacting with teachers and other students. The schema started forming even before you entered school based on the information you got about the school from your parents, your siblings, and the images you saw from different forms of media.

For example, you learned that a ruler, a notebook and a pen are associated with the learning environment. With time, you found out about new concepts like recess, grades, homework, taking tests and studying. You also developed relationships with your classmates, teachers, janitors, and administrators. As your education progressed, so did your schema.

The ease or the difficulty of revising or re-evaluating a schema varies from one person to another, and from one situation to another. For example, some students do not experience any problems changing their schemas as they move from one education level to another, even as their expectations of academic and behavior engagement change. Others do not have a smooth transition because they experience problems interpreting new information using the old yet incompatible schema.

Most of us have been in situations like these when we encountered mistakes, frustrations and disappointments revising our schemas but we eventually learned how to do it right. Being able to adapt your schema is a sign of cognitive complexity and cognitive growth, which is an essential part of life. Therefore, even if a person encounters challenges and makes mistakes, it is alright because the person is in the process of learning and growing.

Being aware of your schemata is important because your interpretation determines how you behave. For example, if you are leading a group discussion and you notice that one of the members is shy, you will instinctively avoid asking him to speak based on your schema about how shy people do not like to talk in public or that they make poor public speakers.

Schemata also guide your interactions and become a script that guides your behaviors. For example, you know how to act on a first date, at a waiting room, in a classroom and even at a game show. A person who has never been in any of these environments will know how to behave.

Schemata are also used to interpret other people's behavior and to form impressions about who they are. This process is aided by soliciting information about the said persons so that we can place the people in a particular schema. For example, in the United States and many other cultures of the West, the identity of a person is closely tied to what the person does for a living. In an introduction, one of the first thing we say about ourselves, or about others is the kind of work we do.

The conversation you have with a person will shift depending on the title the person introduced to you has. For example, the conversation you have with a doctor is different from that which you have with an artist. We often make similar distinctions based on a person's gender, culture, and other factors that could influence perception.

In summary, the schemata guide our interpretation of people, individuals, things, and places, which filters the information and perception we have before, during and after an interaction. The schemata are stored in our memories and are retrieved whenever we need to interpret behavior, and all other stimuli around us. Just like apps are updated when a new version is created, the schemata are updated as we encounter new experiences in life.

How to Interpret Verbal Communication

A young student has worked over 20 hours to complete a 40-page essay for her college class. She then had to develop a visual representation to accompany her presentation. After three restless nights and countless cups of coffee, she is finally ready to present her finished report to the class. After performing an engaging and educational discourse, she breathed a deep sigh of relief. After class, she approached her professor and asked him how he enjoyed it. Barely looking up from his computer, the professor stopped and said, "It was fine," in a monotone voice. She was devastated. After dedicating all of her time and resources to this project, she was not satisfied with, "It was fine." A week later, after wondering what she could have improved upon, she finally got her grade back. Shaking, she opened the link and saw a 100% grade. She was ecstatic. She felt greatly accomplished and proud of her work. However, she still wondered why the professor gave her that response if he was going to give her an A.

The professor could have genuinely loved her presentation. In fact, it could have given him chills. However, because he was so monotone in his response, the student grew insecure. He gave off the impression that he did not appreciate all of her hard work. In reality, the professor greatly enjoyed it; so much so, he gave her a perfect grade. What is the issue with his actions?

Likely, you would conclude that the way he uttered, "It was fine," was a turn off. That monotone delivery is quite different from the excited, "It was fine!" paired with a clap. This is the power of verbal communication. Although one person may say one thing, the way they speak it reveals the truth. Our body language works closely with the manner in which we speak. A rather rude comment can be overlooked when paired with a smiling face, or it could be taken as extremely creepy. In addition, a smile can hide insidious intentions. This is why body language is a compilation of various components.

When a person constantly speaks in a harsh, assertive, and bold manner, others may conclude that that person is angry. They may even avoid associating with them for fear of embracing negative energy. In reality, the person could be amicable and positive. However, the way they place great emphasis on certain words or topics is intimidating. The power of tone, emphasis, and volume can create great conclusions when it comes to reputation. However, there are exceptions to this theory. Some individuals may express themselves one way, yet their actual personality is quite different. Take, for example, the late Michael Jackson. Michael had an extremely light and timid voice. He would speak almost like an unsure child, retelling a bedtime story. Upon only hearing him, one may conclude that Michael was submissive, shy, and quiet. The reality of his persona was quite different. The innovation found within his music and the creativity exuded through his dance moves illuminated great power and confidence. Despite the volume, tone, and inflection of his voice, he was a mighty lion when it came to his craft. Personal friends and family members, however, knew that somewhere, deep inside, lived a submissive, shy, and quiet person. This denotes that within our voice, despite intention, lie deep-rooted personality traits that we may be blind to. The loud and boisterous individual may be seeking to compensate for a deep insecurity. The arrogant and assertive lawyer may be fuming with angry emotions. The way in which a person speaks is complex and reveals truth.

The power behind how you say something can turn your innovative idea into a passed opportunity. Imagine pitching an idea for a new innovation with a monotone voice and no sign of excitement. Surely, those on the other end would not be convinced this is your passion. You may have missed your opportunity simple because you lacked enthusiasm. Your voice can also be a manipulative tool used to assert to others. There is a stark distinction between yelling rules and explaining them. The way a person says something can make a difference in how the sentence is perceived. A stressed manager can assert, "Why are you always late?" to an employee with a stern voice and a frowning mouth. Or she could kindly say, "Why are you always late?" with a slight touch on the shoulder and a concerned tone.

This could be the moment where the employee either opens up or seeks further employment. When you think about it, words are just extensions of the mind. We all use them and express ourselves in one way or the other. However, the tone can drastically alter our perceived intentions and even our reputation.

The volume in which one speaks can ignite action. A whisper may indicate confidential information, while a loud yelp could signal, "Get away." In addition, a monotone voice could indicate disinterest where an emphasis on words and syllables could signal excitement. Sarcasm, on the other hand, is quite tricky to decode as it is subjective to the person speaking. One lively individual could show sarcasm in the same manner they would offer a greeting. This is where contextual clues come into play. Analyze the person's body language. Do they have a slight smile or a straight face? Does what they say seem outlandish in relation to the topic at hand? Interpreting sarcasm involves integrative techniques to understanding. It is a complex system that is unique to each person. One of the primary reasons why sarcasm is so difficult to understand for some is because it can mimic traditional body language cues. In this respect, it may be essential to get to know the person you are speaking with, so they can better understand your personality. Then, little by little, bring on the sarcasm!

Understanding your personal inflection can affect your reputation. You may have the purest of intentions, but your diction, volume, and choice of words is taken adversely. Others may create a distance between themselves and you due to this inconsistency. Being cognizant of the way you say something can be a true indicator of your intention. In addition, your communication skills will operate smoothly. The two main components of mastering effective communication are control and awareness. It is important to control the tone, inflection, and volume of your voice. It may even be necessary to control the type of words you use. Next, being aware of your audience, surroundings, and mood can play a huge role in how your words come off. A bad or melancholy mood may not be suitable for a children's book reading at the library. You can practice altering your verbal skills by seeking feedback from others. Have them analyze how you express a sentence, and they can provide constructive ways to improve.

Chapter 4 Dangers of inaccurate perception

Unfortunately, many missed opportunities, acts of violence, and lapses of judgment occur due to inaccurate perception. Many people lose the opportunity to connect with others because they rely so heavily on initial judgment. Perception is defined as, "the ability to see, hear, or become aware of something through the senses." We gather conclusions about people from the information we receive from them. If we have a negative encounter, likely, we will perceive that person in a bad light. Body language and perception are the two components that equal a conclusion. The way someone positions themselves, holds their hands, or even moves their eyes can be taken a certain way. Although perceiving body language is a natural part of social development, perception can always be altered. We have the grand ability to be able to acknowledge something without jumping to conclusions. Is this really possible when interpreting body language?

Absolutely! One of the primary keys to building understanding is letting go of preconceived associations. For example, a young woman is always standing with her hands crossed, eyes lowered, and mouth downturned. Upon looking at her, you could conclude that she is prudish, stuck up, and distant. This may prevent you from speaking to her. In reality, the young woman is far from stuck up. Rather, she suffers from social anxiety and is uncomfortable in large crowds. She has a fear of carrying on a conversation along with personal insecurities. She desperately wants to make friends but doesn't want to make the first move. This disconnect creates a whirlwind of false notions that prevents pure human connection. Since one person perceives her as being stuck up, they avoid sparking a conversation without truly getting to know her personality. This occurs often and is the result of misunderstandings.

Breaking down those preconceived notions about certain behavior involves eliminating one-way thinking. As opposed to assigning only one meaning to a specific body movement, open your mind to the possibility of other reasonings behind behavior. Environmental factors may even alter traditional body language meanings. Crossed arms usually translate to feelings of self-consciousness or disapproval. However, in an extremely cold room, does it have the same meaning? When talking with a friend during a sunny day, does their looking to the side mean they are lying? Or could the sun be extraordinarily bright? Situational factors are also imperative to drawing definite conclusions. Breaking eye contact doesn't automatically mean your friend isn't interested in your conversation. Perhaps they are fatigued or swamped with personal issues at the moment. It's important to be flexible with how you perceive behavior. By understanding that there is always a reason behind everything, you will learn to give others the benefit of the doubt.

The traditional saying, "You can't judge a book by its cover," is vital to making social connections. A woman with scrunched brows, a downturned mouth, and hooded eyes may give off the impression that she is always angry. However, upon getting to know her, you realize she is extremely friendly. Perhaps that is the natural structure of her face. The same rings true for a man who engages in deep eye contact, leans in towards his subjects, and touches hands as he speaks. These clues may indicate that he is romantically interested in whomever he is talking to. In reality, that may be his way of showing interest in the conversation. It could almost be likened to respect.

Cultural differences may influence how we perceive certain behavior. For example, in the United States, we typically nod our head signifying, "Yes." However, in Greek cultures, a head nod means "No." In Portugal, individuals may tug their ears when something tastes delicious. Comical, yet true, Italians interpret this as a suggestive move with sexual undertones. Europeans kiss openly in public, whereas traditional Asian countries view this as inappropriate in public. The man mentioned earlier whose mannerisms may be suggestive probably grew up predominantly around women. His mother, no doubt, taught him how to show respect and interest to those to whom he is speaking. Although his actions came off as flirtatious, he was simply acting on a natural impulse. When analyzing others, it's key to remember that everyone comes from a different family that implemented different expectations for behavior.

Some families may communicate through touching and warm embraces while another maintains a respectful distance. Before taking offense, consider how they grew up in conjunction with their personality. Perhaps they truly like you, and they are showing you in their own unique way.

Another key way to destroy perception from initial judgment is to get to know the person. Sure, someone may come off as rude, shy, aloof, or even angry. However, are they less deserving of having a social connection with you? Have they done anything concrete that prevents you from associating with them? The initial breaking of the ice may be challenging, but the results are worth it. When approaching someone who gives off negative body language, it's important to consider these tips if attempting to make a connection:

- Ask them about their interests.

- Discuss commonalities and attempt to make a connection.

- Ask them about their family. Do they have siblings? Is their family near or far?

- Share something special about yourself. This may open the door for further conversation.

- Simply ask them how their day is going.

There are a plethora of ice breakers that can be used to approach someone who may seem unapproachable. By doing so, you will learn that, although perception is key, understanding is what shapes relationships. You could be passing up on a purposeful friendship because of a misunderstanding. By taking the additional time to understand someone else, you will then understand their body language. You will learn what encompasses their inner being. This will help you to develop an open mind when building relationships.

Reading People through Their Environment

A person's immediate environment can reveal a lot about his or her, and I don't mean the pop psychology quizzes that keep pooping on your timeline. I mean it is a solid, scientific way to make educated guesses about a person's character. There are psychological principles behind analyzing a person's behavior through his or her immediate environment.

Here are a bunch of awesome, proven tips for reading a person through his or her surroundings.

Colors

The first thing you notice when you enter someone's home is the colors used in the décor. A person's choice of colors can psychologically reveal several aspects of their personality. For instance, if the person is using a lot of bright, bold colors such as red, orange, electric blue, etc., he or she is unafraid to take risks or articulating their thoughts. Their personality is bolder, outgoing and adventure bitten. They are not afraid to say things as they see it.

Subtle colors may imply that the person is more subtle, restrained and reflective in nature. They may be deep thinkers who weigh all options carefully before taking an important decision.

People who are more focused inwards or introverts tend to do up their homes on solid, soft hues and more muted patterns, while outgoing personalities tend to use bold, experimental designs.

The Hidden Closet

The mess in your house probably reveals the mess in your head too! No, that's not being judgmental. It is a way to analyze how people's thoughts and mind leads to the creation of their environment. A neat, organized, efficiently categorized work desk is a sign of a mind that possess great clarity of thought. Excessive cleanliness or orderliness can also be a sign of anxiety, nervousness or low self-esteem. It can also point to a mental health issue such as obsessive-compulsive disorder. Watch out for signs of extreme orderliness and an obsession with cleanliness.

On the contrary, people whose spaces are more chaotic and disorganized looking can reveal a cluttered and disorganized mind. It can be a sign of being good at many things or multitasking. When you are engaged in too many activities, you barely have the time to organize your space, which means it is often left unattended or in a disorganized manner. Sometimes, it can be a sign of plain laziness or lack of clarity/objectives in life.

It has been observed that people with a more extrovert personality tend to have more chaos around them. Their drawers will most likely be messy and disorganized. On the contrary, people who are more reflective and introvert by nature will spend more time meticulously organizing, arranging and prioritizing their belongings.

A majority of people (however picky about cleanliness) have some areas of the home that are a hidden mess. Think under the bed or behind their closets. These are mostly areas that are not often accessed by people and therefore neglected. If a person keeps even these inaccessible areas neat and organized, they may be suffering from anxiety. These are the most likely the type of people who are control freaks or are obsessed with being completely in control of everything around them.

Studies also reveal that a messy, disorganized and erratic environment is a sign of high creativity. People living in such places tend to generate better and more path-breaking ideas. So yes, the cliché about an artist of scientist/inventor with messy hair and a disorganized look is actually true from the psychological perspective.

Prints

Amusing as it sounds, I can tell a lot about a person simply by looking at the prints they use in their décor or on their clothes. Big, bright and bold prints reveal that the person is more self-assured, confident and not inhibited by other's opinion of him or her. They are most likely fiercely independent in thought and action, and original thinkers. They have their own clear opinion/views on several issues and aren't easily influenced by others.

Similarly, quirky prints such as polka dots or animals or comic legends can reveal a fun, whimsical, creative and original personality. Geometric prints, on the other hand, reveal a need for order and organization.

A study conducted by researchers at Yale concluded that people who spend a long time on showers and bathing are mostly lonely. They use the warmth of the bath as a substitute for the lack of emotional warmth.

Psychologists have also deciphered the meaning of having a wall filled with motivational quotes, messages, and posters. According to experts, this is most likely an indicator of neuroticism. These folks use their immediate environment to soothe their nerves and help them sail through. Don't immediately conclude something is wrong with a person or that he/she needs help if they have a wall full of motivational posters.

Talk to them more to gain a better understanding of their personality or observe them closely to gather non-verbal clues.

Old Items

People whose spaces are filled with items from the past such as old job uniforms, sports team jerseys that no longer fit, clothes that they've outgrown, etc. are the ones who most likely live in the past or are unable to let go of their past. They cling to memories and often refuse to move on. Hoarding things belonging to their past is not a sign that they are attached to the belongings per se. These people are in fact clinging to the memories associated with these belongings.

Chapter 5 Emotional intelligence

The term emotional intelligence refers to the ability of an individual to recognize and differentiate between different emotions within themselves and also among other people. The term is also used to describe the utilization of emotional information to make decisions and adapt to their immediate surroundings.

In a nutshell, the term refers to the fact that an individual can appropriately manage their emotions without allowing them to overcome them. This is an important aspect of self-awareness because it allows you to communicate and interact without losing your cool.

Emotional intelligence has been a cause for most peoples' abilities to adapt to their surroundings appropriately and make credible decisions based on how they assess the reactions of those who are around them.

When you are emotionally intelligent, it becomes difficult for you to harbor strong feelings that even affect your thought processes and limit your interactions with other people.

In fact, it allows you to behave in the most appropriate manner and adapt to every single situation without letting any of your emotions dominate your thought processes. It is an effective way of interacting with other people because you can match their feelings appropriately.

For instance, if you are emotionally intelligent, it is not easy for you to lose your cool when other people are angry. Depending on the circumstances, it is possible for you to avoid getting angry when everybody else is upset.

You will be the guiding factor among your friends as you will be able to reason with the situation at hand. If there is something that is affecting your friends and everybody is upset, you will be the voice of reason and guide your friends towards thinking differently from the rest.

The subject of emotional intelligence contains five major aspects, according to The American psychologist Daniel Goleman. These elements are expounded below.

#1 Motivation

You will find that an emotionally intelligent individual is able to motivate themselves aptly without requiring the assistance of other people. They are able to spur themselves into action without having to invoke any outside help.

They understand themselves very well, and they know how to control their most sincere emotional reactions. This means that when it is time to get something done, they are able to do it without relying too much on external factors to motivate them.

If you are able to motivate yourself, you give yourself a great advantage over anybody else because you do not have to seek solace or psyche from anywhere else. Your motivation and inspiration comes from within, and you are able to act accordingly.

Motivating yourself is a very good way of being in control of yourself, and it shows a tremendous level of self-awareness within you. This way, you can approach different challenges with ease without allowing your emotional reactions to get the better of you.

#2 Self Awareness

People with high emotional intelligence do not let their feelings rule over their lives; instead, they are able to discern between different emotions and react accordingly depending on their goals and ambitions.

They do not need other people intruding in their lives and telling them how to behave because they already have a pretty clear understanding of how they should behave. They are in total control over their lives, but it does not mean that they cannot make mistakes.

Instead, they are able to tell even when they are wrong because they have a high level of self-awareness, and they can look at each of their actions in an objective manner. A high emotional intelligence quotient in an individual allows them to behave differently and independently.

When you have a high level of self-awareness, it becomes easy to control your emotions because you do not allow them to drag you down. Instead, you can make tough decisions without being fazed, and you know exactly how to react when trouble comes along.

A high level of self-awareness brings out a much more controlled way of controlling your emotions. You are able to hide your anger and even happiness when need be, and you understand how to deal with other people, as well.

#3 Empathy

People with a high level of emotional intelligence have a lot of empathy for those around them. Empathy can be described as compassion or understanding for those around you, and it allows for better interactions because other people can see that you care for them.

Empathy allows people to like you, and highly emotionally intelligent people always display it even when they are in a bad mood. It is possible for you to have experienced a major loss in your life, but you do not even show it when you are with other people.

Instead, you interact with them in a simplistic and straightforward manner without them ever knowing that you have problems. You tend to their needs and even provide advice in their lives that helps them handle the problems that they are currently experiencing.

When you show empathy, you are able to solicit great friendships because people can immediately recognize your actions and associate them with your selfless character. They are able to like you because you respect them tremendously even if you have your own problems to deal with.

#4 Self Regulation

The term self-regulation refers to the ability to control yourself and emotions without letting them interfere with your interactions with other people and even communication. Self-regulation follows a pattern of control in your life where you already understand exactly how to behave and react to specific situations.

When you can self regulate, you show a high level of emotional intelligence because it means that it is difficult for others to deter you from your actions. You are able to make appropriate decisions based on what you want to achieve and where your life is heading.

In such a situation, you are able to set an example for the people around you because they can associate a calm and controlled personality with your own. People start to emulate you because you have a high level of control over your feelings.

This allows you to have better self-awareness and in turn, you are able to interact with people in a whole different way. You have the ability to mirror their own feelings and even improve the moods of other people whenever you hang out with them.

#5 Social Skills

Emotional intelligence is ultimately characterized by excellent emotional control that allows you to interact with other people in the best possible way. It becomes possible for your friends and even business partners to notice a highly self-controlled individual.

This makes it easy for people to interact with each other, communicate, and even share ideas without feeling weird in any way. Even if you are interacting with customers and trying to sell specific goods and services, they are able to relate with you appropriately because you can match their emotional reactions.

Having excellent social skills is possible even for an introvert because it shows a high display of emotional intelligence. You do not ever let your feelings intrude in your life even when you have been wronged by somebody else; instead, you are able to stay on the path towards achieving your objectives.

Social interactions that are successful show that an individual is capable of understanding the people that they hang out with, even in business. This is important because it also shows that they understand themselves very well as much as they try to understand everybody else in the most realistic manner possible.

There are a number of advantages of having high emotional intelligence when interacting with the rest of the world. There have been some criticisms with regard to the models of emotional intelligence that have been suggested by psychologists from around the world.

This is because it is deemed impossible for somebody to be completely in control of their feelings at all times. There are different circumstances that occur in life that can bring the worst of our emotions, even when we have a high level of self-awareness.

However, despite the criticisms, the fact remains that being in control of your emotions is an important step to analyzing other people. It is not possible to successfully analyze an individual, for whatever reason, if you cannot analyze and control yourself.

Improve Intimate and Family Relations

When you have a high level of emotional intelligence, one of the very first advantages is that you can relate with your family in the most appropriate manner possible. Most people underestimate the power of family because they might believe that hard work is everything.

Love is a crucial thing for anybody in a family because it guarantees a high sense of unity that allows for a happy life. Most happy people in the world have strong family relations that allow them to derive love from a specific place and in turn, remain happy in the long term.

Intimate relationships are also improved drastically when you have a high sense of emotional intelligence because you can set an example for you and your partner to follow. It becomes easy for both of you to discuss your feelings and make appropriate decisions for both of you.

When you are able to discuss your feelings with somebody close to you that you are sharing an intimate relationship, the chances of it ever failing are reduced drastically. You are able to charter an appropriate course for both your lives, and you can look forward to an exciting future together.

You Can Flourish Psychologically

Another crucial advantage of high emotional intelligence is that you remain psychologically happy with your life, and it becomes very difficult for any form of sadness to constantly dominate your life.

High emotional intelligence is closely linked to high life satisfaction because you are in a position to guarantee your own happiness. You do not rely on outside help for emotional balance because you can control your own feelings and make good decisions.

In turn, you can also assess the psychological well being of those around you because you are able to have a slight understanding of what is happening in their lives and you can make appropriate decisions with regard to how you interact with them.

Highly emotionally intelligent people can easily analyze other people because they have a tremendous understanding of their own emotions and reactions. They rarely feel insecure in their lives, and they are able to have a high sense of self-esteem whenever they embark on any type of project.

Positive Perceptions by Other People

This is another important advantage of people with high emotional intelligence because they are in a position to positively influence those around them. If you are constantly in control of your emotions, you can intermingle with other people in a good way.

Imagine somebody who is unable to control their emotions and is constantly angry about something that is happening in their lives. It becomes very difficult to interact with such an individual because their communication will always be focused on the thing that is making them upset.

Somebody with a very low sense of emotional control will constantly let their upsetting lives intrude into friendships and even businesses. This is because it will be the dominating point of conversation and will interfere with the normal relations established among friends.

You will find that when you have a high level of emotional intelligence, the perceptions of those around, you will be that of a highly empathetic, pleasing, and socially skilled person to be around. It makes the process of intermingling much simpler.

This improves your relationships with other people and allows you to bond with other people with similar levels of emotional intelligence. This is quite advantageous as it enables you to analyze people much easier and create new friendships when need be.

You Can Relate With Fellow Adults Appropriately

High emotional intelligence allows your interactions with fellow adults not to be mired in conflict and interpersonal aggression. Instead, it allows for candid interactions where there are meaningful exchanges and appropriate ways of sharing the problems that might be existing in your lives.

Your interactions with fellow adults will mean everything because it is the one way you can command respect from those around you. Correspondingly, you can analyze people in an appropriate manner and be able to choose your friends wisely.

When you have high emotional intelligence, you are able to have a better perception of yourself, which is crucial when you want to motivate yourself and work towards your goals. This is a necessity when you also want to analyze other people for whatever reason.

Excellent relations with fellow adults have a tremendous influence on your social status. When you can interact in a mature way and mirror the feelings and reactions of your fellow adults, you are able to live much more comfortably and achieve happiness in your life.

You Have Better Interactions With Children

You will find that it is much simpler for you to have better social interactions with your children as well as other young ones in the community when you have a high level of emotional intelligence. This is because you can make them happy in the same way that they bring a smile on your face.

Good social interactions with children determine your social status in the community, as well. This is because managing children is very important in guaranteeing that there is always happiness in a family.

You can always suspect something to be wrong whenever you are unable to interact well with children because it is a play on your own emotional reaction. Even children sometimes can see when an adult is upset and unable to control their own emotions, and they will avoid such a person.

As a parent, you must have a high level of emotional intelligence because children sometimes can be a handful, and they can easily upset you. When you identify the basic tenets of making your children happy, you also become happy because it is impossible for their immature behaviors to upset you significantly.

Instead, you will actually embrace their actions, even when they misbehave and you can put it down to the learning process. Better interactions with children are also another way of assessing your own ability to analyze the people around you.

Academic Challenges Can Be Handled With Ease

High emotional intelligence is also related to actual intelligence itself because it determines the manner in which you gain new information in your life. It becomes possible for you to learn new things with ease because you are in full control of your emotions.

Emotional intelligence is related to academic excellence because it allows you to focus on the process of gaining new information and conducting research with minimal distractions. It allows you to focus your energy on what really matters.

According to teachers, students with a high sense of emotional intelligence are always good in class. Although this is subject to their IQ levels, highly emotional intelligent people will always be good in class because they can focus on what really matters.

Imagine if you do not have full control over your emotions, and you are constantly thinking about things that are troubling you. It becomes very hard to learn because there are always emotional problems dominating your thoughts and discourages you from achieving your true potential.

You Gain a High Level of Self-Compassion

Self-compassion is an important attribute for anybody who has a high level of emotional intelligence. It leads them to live happier lives, and they are able to make decisions not based on their feelings but using rationale and their actual needs.

Controlling your emotions allows you to appreciate yourself much more than a depressed person might do. They are able to make conscious decisions that have far-reaching positive effects not only on their lives but also the people around them.

Consequently, they have a much better understanding of themselves, and in turn, they have a much better understanding of the people around them. As mentioned earlier, the analysis of other people around you must begin with an objective analysis of yourself.

When you have a high degree of self-compassion, it becomes very difficult to live a life of depression. You will always be able to see the positive aspects of life and make decisions based on the good-natured feeling you will always have within you.

High emotional intelligence is an important step towards understanding other people because it shows that you are paying adequate attention o your own affairs first. Other people will appreciate this, and it will make it easier for them to mingle with you.

Work Performance Improves Tremendously

When you are emotionally intelligent, not only can you concentrate on your work and guarantee high yields, but you can also interact with the employees around you appropriately. This is quite important if you are to achieve success in your professional life.

As for marketers or any profession that targets new clients to a business, prospective clients will appreciate speaking with a professional who displays a high level of emotional intelligence. This is because they can ask questions and gather as much information as possible on prospective products or services they want to purchase.

Successful marketers always display high levels of emotional intelligence, and this is the primary factor that allows them to analyze other people. Generalized marketing, where a marketer approaches a general audience, might not yield the same success as targeting a niche market.

Success in business requires a cool head and a proper understanding of customers in order to convince them into sales. Success is achieved because it is possible to establish good relationships with customers right from the get-go.

How to Avoid Mistakes?

Mistakes. You think about them, talk about them, and lastly obsess regards to them. These mistakes help a human being to grow but, side by side they are very much embarrassing, shameful, and put companies to a great loss.

Everyone has the same old habit which they want to change by doing some mistake or the other. Actually, it is a part of human psychology to repeat the same behavior again and again. Therefore, changing the old behavior can be difficult but not impossible. It can only be eradicated by proper planning and staying positive while doing any work.

In human life, mistakes are very common things by which he/she learns a lot.

Sometimes when we work too much, some careless and silly mistakes will happen especially when you are doing your best. There isa number of examples of mistakes like sending an e-mail to the wrong person, overlooking a balance sheet, not ready for a presentation, and innumerable others.

Indeed, the person who is good at analyzing people easily judges whether the person has done some mistake or not by non-verbal communication channels.

Here you will come to know "How to avoid mistakes at work"?

First of all, acknowledge a mistake

Until and unless you fully appreciate what exactly has happened, till then it is impossible to avoid it. Some of the individuals are very hard at failure but forgot to re-examine what is to be done to avoid the mistake next time. So, keep these things in mind before doing any work: -

Don't be overconfident while doing any work as it leads to missing any information and you will tend to make a mistake

There are many bad habits which can be the reason of mistake so avoid any bad habit

Doing mistake means you are trying your best but do overdo it

Concentrate on what you are doing

Just focus on your own tasks and projects firsts. At the office, make work your priority and avoid any kind of activity while doing office work. On the other hand, don't be a multitasked as it kills the overall productivity.

Moreover, start the work from the smallest and easy task and then take up a tough one.

Furthermore, at the start of the day give importance to those tasks which are significant.

Don't fear mistakes

This is one of the essential points in order to keep away from doing mistakes. Actually, the reality is in the fear of making a mistake, you try to be perfect but forget that by mistakes only you learn a lot.

In a study, it is considered that the human brain before doing any work sends a warning signal to prevent us from repeating the same mistakes again and again.

However, making mistakes is a good thing which eventually gives an opportunity to analyze themselves and others; but, up to some limit. So, do your work keeping past mistakes in mind.

Avoid distraction

Don't get distracted while doing any of the work in the office as it is prone to mistakes. Actually, distraction can take away your attention and make you jump between the task and the project. On the other hand, it also lowers down the overall productivity from your behalf.

Moreover, they create confusion and your attention will get split between two works. One essential step while doing office work is just put your phone aside as it is one of the most distracting things because of which end number of mistakes can happen.

Take the breaks at the appropriate time

If you work continuously then, it will harm your brain and it will not function in the right way. According to Harvard Business Review, if the person does overwork then the aging process will move faster, which as a result impact on memory and thinking skills.

So, to avoid this take some precautions like: -

Take some break while doing work and relax for some time

Talk to friends and relatives as it makes your brain relaxed and offer you a positive attitude of doing work

When you take a break in work, do something refreshing as it will activate your brain

Ask doubts and questions

The main reason formaking a mistake is having doubts about the assigned work because of their ego or are too afraid of asking. Most of the individuals think that what other people will think if they ask any doubt; but, they forget that if they do some mistake what another person will say about you. Now you can well assume that which one is essential for you.

Therefore, try to ask whatever comes in your mind with regards to the work. This, in turn, will be helpful in learning more about the task and can be very useful in completing your work on time without any mistakes.

Try to make a checklist

Checklists will help you to keep in track all the steps which you will do while completing a task. By following this process, your work will be full-fledged without any errors because you have taken care of every step by rechecking them again and again.

This checklist is also crucial for those individuals who are multitaskers and want to do multiple works at the same time. For them, it is very essential. And one of the crucial things in multiple tasking is don't leave any work incomplete otherwise you will lose the grip on that work.

Do external proofreading on your behalf

As an individual, if you have given your best in doing work then also cross-check the work again and again so that there are no chances of mistakes.

Try to analyze your work by taking the help of your manager, supervisor, or any experienced colleague.

Notwithstanding, getting a second eye on the work is a good method of improvising your work. And also, they make you understand overlooked errors which you are not able to understand.

Be clear with regards to your role in the organization

Do you know- what is the role you have been given by your company?

It is very essential to know this otherwise you will mess up all the things in order to complete every task.

On the other hand, surety of work offered to you makes you comfortable and that work will be mistake-free.

However, if you have any doubt about your duties and responsibilities then ask your boss to define it, and after that things will work much easier. In this case, there are no chances of errors.

Learn from every mistake which you will do

In case any mistake is done by you, don't blame it on others rather take the responsibility of that mistake for what you have done.

As an employee of any organization, learn from every error done by you and from others. Always make a note of all the mistakes done by you and by your colleagues and do the best effort not to repeat it again. Moreover, when you show a positive attitude towards the mistakes, then it will become a stepping stone of your success.

Indeed, this process makes you analyze yourself and others which are best for making strong relationships.

Always find the root of the mistake

Every human being makes mistakes but once it is done, taking precautionary measures so that it will not repeat again is mandatory.

If you want that this mistake will not happen again, then try to find out the root cause of the mistake.

After that think deeply about that issue and what are the steps you can take to prevent it further in the future. This will also help you to analyze your capability to get successful in life while observing others.

Try to have a healthy conflict

Mistakes are done by a single human being; but, in some cases, it might be due to conflicts between colleagues because of clashes in ego and opinions.

Make sure that you build a healthy relationship with each other so that every solution can be sought with the help of colleagues. Make yourself friendly and make a good rapport within the organization.

We all are human and mistakes are our part of life. The person who learns from the mistakes and tries not to repeat it is the best human being. So, with your own mistakes, you can analyze other individuals also the way they react and act to the mistakes and judge their personality.

Chapter 6 Reading into the matters of the heart

Reading into the matters of the heart is tricky business. Even people you love have reasons for withholding information or seemingly spinning the truth. Imagine how hard it would be for your significant other to plan surprises for you if you knew every single time they were hiding something.

On the matter of hidden intentions, even when devoted to others, individuals may still want some semblance of privacy. Having privacy does not equate to devious behaviors. So, before you start to delve into reading the matters of the heart, try to remember trust is essential.

Whether you've just started dating your significant other or you've been together for a while, chances are you know their baseline behavior. All incongruences should be compared to their baseline. If you're going to use this section to determine whether or not someone is interested in you, it's advisable to pick up on their personality type and establish a baseline. – Individuals who are nervous and trying to impress another may exhibit more nervous tendencies making it arduous to determine a baseline.

Lying and Cheating

The sad truth is that sometimes significant others lie. Lies aren't always indicative of earth-shattering news. In relationships, fear could be a prime motivator for deceit. For instance, your significant other (SO), could be afraid to disappoint you, afraid of what you'll think of them, afraid they haven't made enough profess for you, or are worried you won't react well to any number of things. Lies may even manifest because you SO hasn't come to terms with something on their own.

Regardless of the reasons, or what lying may indicate, you'll want to know why your SO is being deceitful. Naturally, you may fear the worst.

You may notice a change in their behavior, or stories that just aren't adding up. If that's the case, it's time to start monitoring their facial expressions, body language, and words. Keep in mind the same tips, one gesticulation is just not enough evidence.

Inconsistencies

Chances are, you know your SO, you may even know them so well they could be an extension of yourself. This prior information is crucial. Inconsistencies in their day to day life, their emotions, their behaviors, are all cues that more is brewing below the surface than they are letting on.

Distance is a telltale sign that your SO may be weavings webs. When people that are usually really intimate start to allow distance to separate them, whether physical, mental or emotional it's a sign that something is going on. For example, if you after work your SO comes home and usually requires twenty minutes to themselves but instead, they take hours where they don't want to talk or be close to you – that's an obvious tell something is amiss. Signs may not always be this obvious but when they are, try not to shrug them off.

Discomfort: If you're with someone, regardless of if it is just dating or something more and your SO shows a level of discomfort around you, or around certain topics that aren't taboo, they may feel awkward trying to hide, hold secrets or even lying to you. Typically, the reason you're dating someone is because you both feel comfortable around each other. Unexplained discomfort is usually a sign that something more is going, and noticing when it occurs will alert you to what may be going on below the surface.

If, they only act uncomfortable with you when you mention, loyalty, or love (and love has already been introduced to your relationship and this isn't a first-time mention) you may want to consider the possibility of infidelity within the relationship or a waning of their emotions towards you. – That isn't to say that at the first sign of discomfort in your relationship you should abandon ship, but you should definitely start investigating subtly and try talking to your partner about what is bothering them.

When you start your conversation be on the lookout for uncommon or unusual expressions for them, for facial cues or body language that may suggest deceit. Finding out your answers could be the same as if you were talking to anyone else.

Awkward Expressions: Chances are you know how your significant other reactions and acts in certain situations. When they smile and how they smile. If you notice that their expressions seemed forced or are awkward, it may be because they aren't as genuine as usual.

Defensive: Another usually blatant sign of manipulation or deceit would be a very defensive SO. Without contrition there is no defensive SO, especially if being defensive isn't usually within their nature.

Unresponsive: Communication has always been key in relationships, a sudden change in how your SO responds to you or if they stop responding altogether, then find out why. Anger is the primary reason to stop communication within a relationship but if your SO just doesn't want to let on to their deceit or discontentment, they may be defensive and unresponsive to questions you ask that would normally

Matters of the Home

When considering matters of your home, there could be more members than just you and your SO. If the two of you have children, other family staying or just roommates, all of these individuals may try to pull some sort of wool over your eyes while they're there.

Your roommate may try to cover up their supposed borrowing of your money, clothes, items or other things. Children may try to get away with breaking the rules and other family members may just try to move about with their own prerogative, regardless of what that is. In situations like these you're at a disadvantage if you can't spot their manipulative behavior and lying cues.

Confrontation

Confrontation of the transgressor can be a tricky situation. These insecurities can create a backlash against you, if you question the transgressor's motive and intentions or try to expose them.

If the person you have caught by surmounting evidence of if you've nabbed them red-handed, then you have to be conscientious of the possibility of an angry response. Those who don't want to be exposed can go to great, even unreasonable lengths to cover up their secrets, as we'll expound upon later, this is essentially how a spouse starts gaslighting.

Being lied to will ruffle anyone's feathers, but don't let it get under your skin when you're approaching the subject. Starting your conversation out angrily will only escalate the matter. So, don't attack your spouse, or anyone in your home, verbally, mentally or emotionally. Approach them openly and benevolently. Try to remain open-minded and ready to understand why they have done what they have done – especially if this is your SO.

In loving, healthy relationships you may find your spouse only lies when they fear disappointing you. If you've taken a loving approach to confronting them about their lie then you may realize how you can help them feel better about these things and prevent the lies from happening in the future.

In the same breath though, there are chronic liars. These are the ones who you can't just forgive and move on in the relationship with as over time the trust the relationship was built on will deteriorate. Simply said, a chronic liar will always have to fight their impulse to lie and you will almost always find yourself on guard about the things they tell you. If you do find a chronic liar in your life, whether your SO, a person in your family or a child, get to know their specific tells, as they may be different from some of the things we've discussed. As you know, they have experience lying and have tried to master the art of getting away with it.

Gaslighting

If you're not familiar with this term, don't worry. Gaslighting is the process of convincing someone that they are crazy, it uses a convoluted combination of manipulation factor to create a desired end result. Gaslighting requires a gaslighter (those who employ this technique of manipulation) to systematically discredit the prey; to do this the gaslighter must first make the prey feel like they themselves may be unstable. This usually spurns from an abuser who wants to make sure their victim cannot seek refuge and won't be believed by friends and family if they ever come forward as having been abused.

This was seen frequently in the times were females were forced to be dependent upon their husbands. Certain husbands wanted to discredit their wives for various reasons and there was no better way to do it than to make everyone, including the wife think that she was crazy. A sad and unfortunate reality. An even more melancholy truth is that this manipulation technique is still used today.

Have you ever been told you're crazy? Chances are you have, but has anyone ever tried and dedicated themselves to convincing you that you were indeed crazy? We find that gaslighters go to insane lengths to convince their victims. In the famous 1944 movie "Gaslight" the husband would do various things, like turning on the lights and then tell his wife that she did it. Of course, because she didn't do those things she had no memory of them, in which case he insisted she did and that she just didn't remember. It's always heartbreaking when someone you love takes advantage of your trust and insists that you're crazy to the point that you believe them. While you may only find dedicated gaslighters to be those who are of the manipulator type or are a sociopath, you as one who has worked to defend against liars and manipulators have to be aware of this occurrence.

Gaslighting don't just tell the prey that they crazy and systematically convince them of it, they will start to tell others that the prey is starting to go crazy. This creates a situation where the friends and family members are concerned, and those friends also try to convince the prey that he/she is crazy or needs help, but it's okay because they want to offer support. These friends and family members are genuinely concerned and have taken the manipulator at face value, they are going to do all that they can to also convince the prey to face the 'reality' of their disorder. This will go on and on, and only get worse as it continues until the prey starts to accept that fact that maybe, they are truly crazy and that's why they don't remember things or that's why strange things are happening. With what seems to be an army against you, there is hardly any way to cling to the real world of what you once knew. The longer this goes on, the further into victory the gaslighter goes, and the further into dread and despair and sadly, acceptance the prey goes.

Be aware that there are people out there who want nothing more than to take advantage of the weak and convince them they're the crazy ones. Use the tips and tricks in this book to identify these individuals and stay clear away from them. Protect your friends and family from them.

If you confront someone about their lies and they try to turn it onto you, they may have gaslighter tendencies. If they are willing to go to seemingly unreasonable lengths; solid advice to take would be to stay away from them.

Chapter 7 Body Language

The secret signs revealed by body language

You get all excited for a meeting with the client and he's face-tight, lips drawn, wrinkles on his forehead and arms crossed.

"Here comes my lead" - you think.

Has that ever happened to you: perceiving by body language what the person you're talking to is thinking?

Have you ever wondered how understanding body language can help you design and implement the sales process?

Here are some body language tips that can help your sales. Body language hides many secrets. The wrong posture can reveal insecurity, fear, mistrust, and more. On the other hand, the correct posture gives the impression of strength, power, and self-confidence. Understand more about how to take advantage of body signals to get the impression you want.

Negative Body Language

Often during a conversation, you can express negative body language without realizing it. Your facial expressions and gestures can end up showing several details. Some negative postures you should avoid in your meetings with clients are:

- Hands on the waist or in the pockets

- Knees pointing to the exit door

- Legs wide open

- Crossed arms

These attitudes are perceived, even if unconsciously, by the other person, and can ruin the progress of a sale. Here are some other signs that you should avoid so that you don't transmit the wrong body language.

1- Hand in the mouth

Expert analysis shows that when a person is not speaking the truth, they usually cover their own mouth. Variations of this type of posture are:

- To pass the hands to the lips

- Touch the chin

- Put objects in front of the mouth

2 - Compressed lips

Another negative body language is to compress the lips. This act demonstrates that the person is trying to avoid saying what he thinks. That is, hiding your lips reveals that you do not want to answer any questions.

3 - Unfocused look

Body language says a lot by looking. An unfocused or upward and right-pointing look indicates confusion. This is because, when looking away, the person is seeking a mental image. Soon, it shows a lack of clarity in his speech and can also show insecurity.

4- Contracted brow

In a conversation, if the other person wrinkles their forehead, this is not a good sign. These horizontal lines show a certain level of tension, doubt, or nervousness which is a bad sign in body language.

5- Restricted hand and arm movements

Staying with your hands behind or glued to the body conveys the message that you have little confidence. Another gesture to be avoided is placing your hands back or feet crossed behind the chair. These are signs of discomfort.

The Body Language of Self-confidence

It is not enough just to understand what should not be done. It is important that your attitude also shows what you want to expose. A body language of power impresses customers, colleagues, and anyone else you interact with. In demonstrating authority, performance in work and personal life tends to increase. Everyone likes to be around someone who feels safe in their own skin. And this is what you will learn. So stay tuned for tips.

1- Be the dominant one in your handshakes

When talking to a business partner or client, pay attention to the time of fulfillment. Much more than a handshake, this gesture shows who dominates the conversation. If you reach down with your palm, it indicates that you are leading the conversation. If you do the opposite, palm up, it shows that you expect the other to take the lead. Using hugs in body language in business is rarer, but it can happen when there is a relationship of friendship and deep fellowship. But be aware: in certain cultures, this is unacceptable.

2- Breathe deeply

The rhythm of one's breathing reveals many signs. By inhaling and exhaling in a superficial and quick way, one gives an impression of stress, nervousness, and fear. If you want to show self-confidence use a technique: take a deep breath until you feel the wider abdomen and the ribs expanding. A slow, deep breath helps control anger and anxiety.

3- Fix your eyes between the other person's eyebrows

Speaking looking into someone's eyes can be difficult for many people. But the way you look at the other shows who is in control of the debate. An easy way to use the power look is to imagine a spot between the person's eyebrows and keep your eyes on that spot. That way, you will be showing security.

4. Talk quietly

The voice is key to getting the right message across. It helps to pass on a sense of credibility and authority. When you are speaking, articulate each word well, pause and breathe quietly between sentences. This ensures that the other person understands what is being said.

5. Look for a neutral stance

Crossed arms indicate annoyance or if someone is closed to the subject. However, keeping the hands at the side of the body, lightly, is a message of neutrality. A good tip is to try to mirror the gestures of those who are talking to you. This creates an atmosphere of sympathy and friendship.

With these body language techniques, you will pass the correct image to your interlocutors. With them, you will greatly facilitate negotiations with your customers and gain respect in your work environment.

Meaning of Corporal Language

What is Corporal Language: Body language is a form of non-verbal communication, where the body "speaks" through gestures, facial expressions, and postures.

Body language arose well before verbal language and still represents one of the most important forms of communication used by human beings. Experts claim that approximately 93% of all human communication is non-verbal. About 55% of communication is done without the use of words, that is, it is related to postures, facial expressions, and gestures. The sonority and vocalization (tone of voice, rhythm, and speech speed) are also important and correspond to 38% of the messages transmitted.

The posture of the arms, legs, head, and facial expression can convey various feelings. For example, if a person does not make eye contact while another person is talking to her, it may mean that she is not interested in the conversation or the person. On the other hand, when a person is holding his arms crossed, this posture can be considered defensive, revealing insecurity. The distance between one speaker and another may also indicate tension between the two.

Social psychologist Amy Cuddy says that our stance can not only change others' opinions about us, but it also influences our view of ourselves. Cuddy also identifies powerful and non-powerful postures that can have a positive or negative impact on our self-esteem. Proper posture can contribute to a number of scenarios, such as job interviews.

Body Language and Lies

There are many experts who are dedicated to the study of body language and can identify the true feelings of a person, which often do not match what the person says.

The American psychologist Paul Ekman is recognized as the greatest specialist in facial expressions. His work influenced the creation of the series Lie to Me, where a trained group solves various crimes by observing the body language of the various suspects. According to some experts, there are 15 signs of body language used to identify a lie.

Body Language and Attraction

Charles Darwin was one of the first to address the body language of some animals when it came to finding a partner. Males often court females, typically altering their behavior to increase their chances of "conquest."

For humans, body language also plays an important role in seduction because the way an individual behaves alters the capacity for seduction. Male and female body language also reveal the availability and interest for a loving relationship or physical involvement.

A man who has a confident and uninhibited posture will probably have a greater capacity for attraction. The success of interactions or flirting is often dependent on the attitude and ability of the subject to interpret a person's body language. For example, if a woman is touching her hair while talking to you, this may be a sign of interest on her part. If a man looks several times directly at you in a short time, this may indicate that he has an interest.

With regard to seduction, it is important to note that male body language is different from female body language. Moreover, even among people of the same gender, there are differences because different personalities result in distinct forms of body language.

Body Language and Gestures

It is important not to confuse body language with sign language. Sign language is more objective, and each gesture has its own meaning, which was established by convention. In body language, a certain posture or gesture is more subjective and may or may not reveal a mental or physical attitude.

9 Tips to Have Confident Body Language

How can one have good body language? There are some people who seem to convey natural and unwavering confidence. They usually stand out in their career, in love relationships, and in any possible social situation. For the rest of us, it is possible to repair our body language. But for most of us, it's not always easy to act with a confident stance in front of others. The good news? Everyone can develop their confidence. And one of the first steps is to change your body language.

It may seem like just one detail but make no mistake: the effect is tremendous. First, with the correct posture, you will transmit signs that will build a more positive image for others, bringing various benefits to your interpersonal relationships. In addition, studies have already proven that body language greatly influences the action of the brain. If you physically behave as a leader, the brain acts accordingly. Madness, right? But it is science.

So, without further ado, ladies and gentlemen, here are 9 tips to show confidence with your gestures:

#1 Keep the Right Posture

Let's start with the basics. Maintaining an upright posture, with shoulders aligned and not bent forward, is the first step to having good body language. If you get all crooked, you'll have a sloppy and narrow image. This goes for when you are standing or sitting as well.

#2 Keep Your Head Up and Look Forward

Now that you've straightened your back and shoulders, it's time to take care of your head. Keep your chin up - without overdoing it, obviously - instead of letting it point your gaze down. Confident people do not stare at the ground but look forward.

#3 Do Not Cross Your Arms

This is a classic gesture people make when they are uncomfortable with a situation. They cross their arms, which is a defensive position. Avoid doing this.

#4 Gesticulate With Your Hands

Gesturing with your hands will help you express yourself better and, in addition, pass an expansive air. A curiosity? One study found that during a speech, charismatic leaders gesticulate four times more with their hands than normal people.

#5 Smile

Ah, the smile. This is a powerful gesture to show others that you are a trustworthy, sociable, and pleasant person. After all, if you're a confident and well-off person, why would you be closed-faced?

#6 Have a Firm Handshake

We have already discussed the art of the handshake in a previous section. The ideal is for the handshake to be neither too strong (to the point of intimidating people) nor too weak (so you do not seem insecure). The key is to find the ideal balance of firmness.

#7 Avoid Gestures of Anxiety

Standing by drumming your fingers - or wiggling your feet while sitting, or scratching your face while talking, etc - are classic signs of nervousness, anxiety, and restlessness. Show that you are sure of yourself through your gestures.

#8 Make Eye Contact

Fleeing from eye contact is an indicator of insecurity. But if you exaggerate, on the other hand, you will look like a maniac trying to intimidate people. The secret is in the middle. Experts suggest looking directly into the other person's eyes around 50% of the time while you talk.

One technique they suggest is to imagine a triangle in the person's face - left eye, right eye, and mouth - then vary your focus between these three points every few seconds.

Of course, it is absolutely normal to look away a few times during the conversation, but always with the expression of who is trying to remember something or reflecting on the topic. Take care not to give off an air of disinterest.

#9 Inspiration from Confident Men

To end our tips, a cool idea is to watch confident men you admire - they can be series/movie characters like Harvey Specter, Suits, or real personalities like David Beckham - and reproduce some of their gestural habits.

Body Language Tips to Identify a Liar

São Paulo - "You may be a very attentive and insightful person, but your chances of catching a liar are relatively low." This is what behavior expert Paulo Sergio de Camargo, says. According to him, a layman in body language is typically only correct 50% of the time he tries to identify a liar by his posture. But even the most experienced experts do not always succeed: their chances of success are usually around 65% or a little more.

The main difficulty lies in the fact that the signs of lying are often confused with vestiges of shyness, anxiety, and nervousness. This is what Camargo calls the "Othello mistake" in reference to the classic character of Shakespeare. Instead of fear, the protagonist of the tragedy sees betrayal in the eyes of his wife, Desdemona, and commits a terrible injustice. In real life, miscalculations are also common - especially if you are emotionally involved in the situation.

One advantage the expert has when analyzing videos or interviewing defendants, for example, is that he does not have a direct relationship with the liar. In everyday work, however, the feelings and expectations you feed your interlocutor may "cloud" your judgment of his honesty - for good or for bad. Still, there are certain classic signs that usually betray liars. For example, scratching the neck, nose, lips or cheek, are all actions that reveal a state of tension, also due to physiological changes caused by anxiety such as heat, itchiness or sweat. The most classic of these gestures is to scratch the nose, which is called significantly "Pinocchio effect".

Chapter 8 Non-Verbal Communication

You probably noticed that people do not always say what's on their mind. Some people say, "Okay, whatever you want" or "Fine. Go ahead" when they actually mean the opposite.

There are also times when you try to guess whether you should really believe someone who says, "I'll think about it." This is especially the case when you are in an industry or field where finding out what really is going on in people's minds can determine how successful you will be i.e. the real estate industry.

All these points to one thing – it helps to know what really is going on in people's minds, and this book will help you do just that.

Analyzing People Is Possible

Let's get this out of the way - this book will not grant you any power to be a mind reader. What it will do is give you tips and tools so you can read behavior and find out what people think. Fact is, you have probably been doing it for a long time - when you have the gut feeling that a person you are talking to is lying, attracted to someone in the room, or is trying to dominate, you have been unconsciously analyzing people and their body language.

Take a look at a silent movie, such as City Lights that starred Charlie Chaplin. In the absence of dialogues, you are still able to follow the story, which in the case of City Lights, a mismatched love story between a vagrant and a blind flower vendor.

When you see this film, you will realize that one of the characters here only recognizes his friend when he is drunk, and Charlie Chaplin's character is able to show that he is in love or that he is having fun. While people are aware that they are merely watching a film, the production of the film made it possible for its audience to suspend beliefs through well-rehearsed nonverbal gestures.

When you think about the past era of films, people are able to follow what happens in a silent film scene simply by observing nonverbal cues and taking clues from the musical scoring. They do not need to hear any verbal line to understand a full length film – they only need to see how the character gestures and reacts. People have been observing nonverbal language in a pop culture setting decades before the notion of body language became a mainstream to the masses.

If you believe that you are "intuitive" or "perceptive" when it comes to judging other people, it means that you have the ability to read non-verbal clues as well. If you have that hunch that a person is lying, you are recognizing that the behavior of that person and his words do not match. You may also have the feeling that you are not getting along well with a person that you are trying to know better and then adjust your movements to make him more comfortable around you.

So what do all these mean?

Here's the answer: People are capable of reading universal behaviors, regardless of culture, race, or language of the person that they are trying to observe. In order to be able to understand these behaviors better, you need to understand what they are trying to represent.

Where Did This Concept Come From?

The idea of reading non-verbal language first became popular when Charles Darwin released a book about it in 1872. Called The Expression of the Emotions in Man and Animals, this work brought forward observations about human beings truly interact with each other, which was validated further during the following century. Albert Mehrabian made it known that a message is 55% non-verbal, 38% vocal, and only 7% words. That means that even if people do not say anything, they would still be able to communicate at a certain degree to others. Researchers also believe that words are only functional when it comes to giving out information, while all non-verbal channels that a person has would be very essential when it comes to negotiating all interpersonal behavior.

Can You Predict Human Behavior?

This is where the gem of analyzing behavior really lies – if you can predict what a person is likely to do next, and then you are very likely to know how you are going to react to get the results that you want from your interaction with another person.

Studies conducted by a team led by Professor Albert-Laszlo Barabási on phone users' mobility patterns revealed that while there is common perception that human actions are unpredictable and totally random, people actually display regular patterns. While the anonymous users they have observed came from different socio-economic statuses, races, genders, occupation, and ages, no matter how different people travel with their phones, they are still able to get behavior prediction of about 93%.

While they assumed that people who tend to travel less away from their home will offer predictability, they concluded that despite heterogeneity of people, everyone can be equally predictable.

What does that say about people, then? Simple: by determining stimulus and observing how people react towards them, you get a better idea about the emotions that drive their actions. While it is not possible to get an actual reading of what people are thinking, you can make deductions on what their thoughts are based on the emotions that they display or suppress.

Benefits of Analyzing People

Being able to understand non-verbal clues will help you do the following:

1. Become aware of possible intentions of other people.

Learning to observe the behavior of people around you would help you decipher information that you may not get from what they would actively say.

2. Learn the appropriate response for behavior that people exhibit when they communicate with you.

People generally do not broadcast their emotions. As a result, observing their actions correctly, will allow you to have an insight into those emotions without actually having to have a verbal conversation. You can then give the best response – the kind that would get you the results you want i.e. a specific action.

3. Detect deceit or manipulation attempts.

One of the perks of understanding non-verbal clues is that you can easily decipher any attempt by any person to lie or manipulate you. This is one of the reasons why that language analysis is used in law enforcement.

4. Make people like you.

By displaying the right non-verbal attitude towards people around you, you would be able to not only communicate better with them, but also display behavior that would make them trust and like you.

5. Understand and manage your behavior better.

At this point, you may not be aware of all the nonverbal cues that you send out, which may result in giving out information that you would rather keep to yourself, such as negative thoughts about yourself or other people around you. While it may not be your intention to deceive others, you are fully aware that not all information is helpful in building a relationship or getting the results that you want.

Knowing more about nonverbal communication gives you the edge of communicating information that works for your best interests.

Roles of Nonverbal Communication Cues

Since the publication of The Expression of the Emotions in Man and Animals by Charles Darwin on 1872, research about nonverbal communication has largely anchored on the idea that humans, through evolution, have developed a seemingly universal language for communicating with each other. This also proves that while people might not be aware that they are communicating with others nonverbally, everyone around them also responds to them unconsciously.

However, if you want to improve how you communicate with others, it is important that you become sensitive to the nonverbal cues that you receive and also to the ones that you send out. For starters, you need to take note of these roles that nonverbal cues do when you relate with other people:

1. Repetition

When you repeat things, verbally or nonverbally, the person that you are communicating with remembers the message that you are trying to deliver better. When you send out nonverbal cues, you tend to repeat any truthful verbal message that you utter.

2. Contradiction

Nonverbal cues are mainly controlled by your subconscious. That means that when you are trying to say one thing verbally that contradicts your real thoughts, you may unconsciously negate the words that you say with your actions. At the same time, the person that you are communicating with may also notice that contradiction and react to your nonverbal cues.

3. Substitution

Since communication rests largely on nonverbal cues and gestures, it is possible for a person to communicate to others without even having to say words. For example, you may be completely aware that a person does not want the food served to him when you see him shake his head towards it.

4. Complementing

Nonverbal cues add content to any verbal message, which increases its impact. For example, congratulating someone and then patting his back makes him feel that your happiness towards his success is beyond what your words can say.

5. Accenting

You can nonverbally stress out important details of what you are saying by doing gestures that may accent your words. For example, pounding on the table or gesturing your hands may send out the meaning to your audience that you are saying and expressing an extremely important point.

6. Transitioning

Nonverbal cues also provide clues on what is going on in a conversation, and is very essential in letting people know that it is their turn to speak or act when they are engaging for others. For example, you may gesture towards a person or pause from speaking to indicate that you are done speaking and you want to hear a response.

Types of Nonverbal Communication

People communicate to one another with the following:

1. Facial expressions

These expressions make up for a huge part of how people communicate nonverbally to one another. With a single frown or smile, or whenever your facial muscles move, you are already conveying a huge amount of information. Also notice that a person's face is the first thing that you notice even before you pay attention to what he is saying.

Facial expressions are also believed to be universal across cultures since the same facial muscles are at play whenever an emotion is triggered in a person. For that reason, a smiling person will always register as a happy person, no matter what his race, gender, or socio-economic status is.

2. Gestures

These are deliberate body signals or movements that convey meaning without any use of words. Gestures include pointing, using fingers to tell a numeric value, or waving. Take note that the meanings of gestures are dependent on the culture that uses it.

Gestures often play an important part in telling a different context from what is being said, or to influence an audience in a nonverbal fashion. For example, lawyers make use of gestures to persuade juries to take a particular side in ruling.

A lawyer may look at his watch or tap his feet fast to indicate that a testimony in a witness stand is unimportant and a waste of time. Because deliberate gestures can affect outcomes and also create unfair advantage, there are even judge rulings that prevent some of these nonverbal gestures in a court.

3. Paralinguistic

Paralinguistic is mainly concerned about the way words are spoken – the tone of voice, pitch, speed, fluency, and word spacing changes the meaning of what is being said altogether. You may notice that you may find a person with a strong, mid-range voice to be more credible than a soft-spoken one, even when they have said the same thing.

4. Posture and Body Language

While the study on body language and posture started fairly late, it was proven that the way a person positions his body can impact the way he thinks and how he is also perceived by other people around him. Further research also proved that body language is also not as definitive as previously believed, and it is displayed with subtlety.

5. Proxemics

The concept of space, or the amount of distance that you need from another person or what you believe you own, is one of the important factors that determine how a person believes. Proxemics is often defined by cultural upbringing, level of familiarity with the environment, social norms, personality, and some situational factors.

6. Eye Gaze

The way a person's eyes behave when engaging with other people can also change the meaning of words that he say, or have an effect on his credibility. At the same time, how a person looks at objects or other people around him can indicate emotions, such as attraction, interest, and even hostility.

7. Haptic

Haptic is a type of nonverbal communication that involves touch. Since all human beings require recognition and/or interaction with others, people are able to tell the kind of emotion that they are receiving from another person by the way they receive touch, or how they are deprived of it.

8. Appearance

While you might believe that you cannot judge a person according to looks, the truth is we do as a person's appearance still communicates with you and affects your judgment about that person. Attorneys and doctors that are rated to have pleasant appearance are more likely to be viewed by their clients to be trustworthy and get return clients. In 1996, a study revealed that lawyers that are said to be more attractive than their peers are paid 15% better by their clients.

9. Artifacts

Objects or images chosen by people to represent themselves also send out a great deal of information. For example, choosing an icon or an avatar for your profile in an online forum will tell other people what your preferences are. Artifacts, such as uniforms, also tell a lot on how a person is likely to behave in a particular situation.

Knowing about these types of nonverbal communication that exists between people allows you to interpret behavior or even predict what a person is likely to do next. These details are wildly used in psychic reading, sales, mentalist, police enforcement, and other fields of interest that involve cold reading or any skill that requires knowing a person and his behavioral tendencies. This information also gives you a lot of advantage when you need to get to know a person better or become better at persuading others!

Nonverbal Communication and Your Behavior

One of the most important reasons on why it is very important to analyze behavior is that the nonverbal language we use is also the language that we use to communicate with ourselves. While we think that the language that we use, nonverbal or not, only goes towards the people that we engage on a day to day basis, this is actually a big fallacy that we kept on holding on about communication. According to studies, people communicate with their selves about 50,000 times a day.

That also means that any individual is their own receiver of the nonverbal gestures that they do, and that intrapersonal communication also makes a person feedback on his own behavior. When you observe your own nonverbal gestures, you would realize that assuming a confident posture even during the times that you are very uncertain about what you would do can in fact make you feel confident.

Now that you know what you are to look for when analyzing people, it's time to get to know the types of nonverbal gestures better.

Chapter 9 Bonding With People (Mirroring Body Language)

Mirroring someone else's body language is something we all do automatically, especially if we want to make a connection with them. Smile and the world smiles with you is closer to the truth than you might imagine. Have you ever felt happy about something, glad to be alive, and walked through the streets with a smile on your face? Did you notice how many people smiled back at you and maybe initiated a conversation? Smiling, like yawning, is a facial expression we all seem to copy without thinking. We might even start talking like them without realizing.

Why do we do it?

Some studies have shown that we have a neuron, which controls recognition of faces, and it is this neuron, which makes us, mirror others' expressions. It is a bonding tool and by mirroring others' emotions, it makes the other person feel as if you are empathic and understand how they are feeling.

Even as early as the womb, the baby's heartbeat beats in rhythm with its mother's. As soon as we are born we begin mirroring the facial expressions and body positions we see. If our mother smiles into our faces, we are more likely to smile back.

How often have you heard someone say to someone else, "You reminded me of your mother/father?" This is because the mannerisms were the same, copied from an early age. It's how we learn our native tongue and develop a local accent. We are bonded into a group identity, which can be assumed in any situation to integrate us within a new group, or even a new one-on-one relationship or conversation.

Of course, it can also work the other way. A baby or toddler feels validated when his parent mirrors his facial expression. So, the mother might say to the baby, "Are you giving me a smile?" and mirror the action. It is in this way that the child learns what the expression is. Without this skill, the child is less able to relate to others and may not develop the emotion of empathy and so is less like to form well-grounded relationships. This is because that when we form relationships we look for things we have in common with others. Similarities help us to form a bond, which is normally reflected in facial expressions and body language. If this is lacking, then it becomes more difficult to find a rapport with others.

Copycat

If a man does this with a woman, she is likely to think that he is caring and intelligent but don't try and fake it and go totally overboard because it could end up being farcical. Can you imagine yourself suddenly adopting an Irish accent for instance? Nevertheless, you might subconsciously notice you have a bit of a twang without even trying. However, you might more easily assume the same body position so if she leans forward on the table, you do the same. If she rests her face on her hands, you do it too.

It's also true that if you adopt a particular body position, say standing with your legs apart, you are likely to start experiencing the associated emotion, so you would begin to feel more confident. Crossing the fingers, which is putting the fingertips of each hand together, shows that the person is confident and relaxed. To effect this emotion, assume this position with your hands and the emotion will become real.

Try to become more aware not just of other people's body language and positions but your own because you can control what messages you are sending out to others. Notice if they copy you. If they do, it means that they want to get closer to you and are trying to understand what you are feeling.

Getting the Girl

Of course, this all changes if a man is in the courtship phase with a woman. If a couple is in love it is quite common for them to mirror each other's actions. They will assume the same body language and facial expressions. The closer the couple become, the more language is mirrored. Even when you are trying to impress someone who you would like to be closer to, this is a useful tactic to employ. Drink when they drink, smile at the same time and they will believe that you have a lot going on and that you just seem so right together and clicked. Put on some music in the background. The beat of the music should mean that you both start tapping your feet at the same time or move with the same rhythm.

The longer a couple stay together, the more likely they are to start looking like each other. Because they are using the same facial muscles to reflect the other, their muscles start developing in a similar fashion. If the mirroring declines over time and turns into a grimace the relationship is more likely to break down. And it will obviously be the one who has the more positive facial expressions who is more likely to notice the decline.

Beware of the Situation

Be aware of who you are with when your body starts mimicking theirs. If you are with your boss and your body is doing the same as theirs, they might think you are impertinent or full of yourself. On the other hand, if you are dealing with some jumped up, pompous fool who thinks that they are better than you go ahead and copy their body language. It will throw them off but be prepared to run too!

Interviews

For instance, if you are going for an interview, quite often interviewers believe they have to adopt a closed, non-committed appearance, which does not reveal their thoughts. They do this so that the interview is not biased towards any candidate and so that everyone receives a fair chance. When you enter the room, be aware that this might be the case and try not to mimic their body language. It will send out the wrong impression. Instead, remember to display open body language. Go in there smiling and make lots of eye contact. If you are convincing, they will begin to adopt your body language and you will know that the interview is going well.

As you gain their confidence and attention, and their body language starts to relax, introduce some mirror images of their body language. If you get them onside you will be able to recognize this, and they will be more likely to help you get what you want: the job, the promotion, the raise.

Crowd Pleasers

It is not unusual for a whole crowd to copy one person's actions. Fans at a concert may leave their seats to stand at the front rather than be the only person sitting. Stadium spectators will start off a wave reaction. Studies have been done to show that people will copy others so that they do not stand out in a crowd. For instance, in a waiting room, if one person took a ticket and then threw it away someone watching might assume that they had to do it too. There might be no obvious reason why, but they may sit there and suppose it triggered some mechanism for instance to place the in a queue. When others witnessed this, they followed suit until everyone who entered was taking a ticket from a machine and throwing it away. All for no reason.

If you want to build a strong report, mirroring is a super powerful way to do it and can improve your relationships across the board. Do it to someone you already know well and see what a difference it can make. It is such a strong tool that it might be best to practice before you try for that promotion using it.

Chapter 10 Determining Personality through Birth Order

Analyzing people through their birth order isn't just a bunch of stereotypes or cocktail party talk but a fairly accurate manner of predicting someone's personality based on their childhood experiences. Our birth order often determines the roles we play in our families or the status quo we are given during our early childhood years, which ultimately shapes our fundamental personality or the way we relate to others.

Even though it seems like a study in pop psychology, subconsciously the way we relate to our immediate family members during early childhood has a deep impact on the way we turn out as adults. Many parents will vehemently confirm the fact that each of the children is different from the other regarding personality, though they are all raised in the same house/environment.

There are several factors that along with birth order determine the personality of an individual, and these factors are so closely woven that they cannot be isolated while studying an individual's personality of his or her birth order. Some of these factors are: number of family members or children in the family, the family's socioeconomic status, the parent's education level, environmental factors, and more.

Alfred Adler (an associate of Sigmund Freud and Carl Jung) was the first to propose the theory of determining an individual's personality through his or her birth order while analyzing his clients. However, it was psychologist Frank Sulloway of MIT who modernized the theory for contemporary application.

In his path-breaking book, Born to Rebel Sulloway named five primary traits that defined a person, which are extraversion, neuroticism, openness, agreeableness, and consciousness. According to him, a person's birth order impacted all these fundamental traits. He made a startling conclusion that people who have the same birth order have more in common personality-wise than siblings who are raised together. This is because, according to him, a person's birth-rank impacts them more than his or her environment.

According to author and parenting expert Grose, two children never assume the same role within a family. We all automatically and instinctively take on roles within groups without realizing it. Our families are often the first group we are exposed to. The dynamics that define the role we take on in the very first group largely influence our personality.

Here are a few tips for reading people through their birth order.

First Born

The stereotype of firstborn individuals is that they are natural leaders, ambitious by nature and innately responsible. This is partly true because for some time the child doesn't have any competition when it comes to earning the affection and attention of family members. They don't have to compete with siblings for time and attention from parents. This gives them a slight edge over siblings.

Again, they tend to be caretakers or surrogate parents for their younger siblings (often teaching them things the older child has learned before, the younger siblings). This makes them develop leadership skills and a more accountable, responsible nature. They are protective by nature, and often lead the way for others.

On the flipside, if parents place great expectations on the firstborn, and he or she feels incapable of matching up to those expectations, they can develop a damaging personality that is marked by low self-esteem, the constant need for validation and acceptance from others, low self-confidence and a general feeling of never being good enough for anything or anyone.

According to Sulloway's research, firstborn showed more signs of conformism for rules and respect for authority/tradition. They demonstrate signs of respecting the established status quo rather than challenging it.

A study about firstborns reveals that they tend to be more goal-oriented and place high importance on success and accomplishments. Their place in the birth order makes them lean towards achievements. The first born's personality may also be marked by a constant need to be control and authority, at times making them appear bossy or dogmatic. They are almost always concerned about other's approval.

As per Sulloway's birth order theory, firstborns who are considerably physically stronger than their younger siblings are likely to demonstrate dominant behavioral traits.

Some typical traits of first-born people are – goal oriented, responsible, determined, conformists and meticulous/detail oriented.

Middle Borns

Middle borns often have a more complex personality because they don't enjoy the special rights of the oldest child nor the leeway or privileges of the youngest child. They are awkwardly juxtaposed between the two, owing to which they turn out to be excellent negotiators or peacemakers. These are also people who have a wider social circle as they rely on friends for attention and support when parents focus more on the youngest or oldest sibling.

In case the oldest child doesn't fit the role of a leader at home, the middle child takes his or her place or fills their shoes. Also, there can, in fact, be several middle children. How does one determine their personality in such a scenario? For example, in a family of five children, there can be three middle children. As a rule of the thumb, each child shows personality traits that are different from the one immediately next to him or her in order. This means that within the three middle children, the first and last will have more similar traits than the middle one.

Middleborns are typically social by nature and are obsessed by a sense of fairness and peace. They are known for their excellent negotiation skills, which make them good diplomats and peacemakers.

While the oldest child enjoys undivided attention from parents, while the youngest can get away with murder, family's middle baby is often left with neither. Since they are literally juxtaposed in the middle, they turn out to be amazing compromisers, peacemakers, and negotiators. These kids are harder to pin down and are more loyal, faithful and relationship-oriented by nature. They seldom let down people who trust them or are close to them.

Middle borns typically display these personality traits – they are peacemakers, flexible, accommodating, diplomatic, free-spirited and magnanimous. They are known to work well in teams and relate well with people who are younger or older to them in age or authority since they have a more amiable nature.

Middleborns are also known to be competent in more than a single skill.

Last Born

The last born is often known to be a charmer and risk taker. They are more free-spirited, creative and adventurous. There is a tendency to reinvent the wheel rather than following established rules and norms.

Parents tend to be less careful and cautious with the last born since they've already lived through the experience of being a parent at least once and aren't as overwhelmed by the prospect as when they became parents for the first time. Also, parents generally tend to be more financially well off than they were during the birth of the first child, which means there is a tendency to indulge the child more.

Parents are more relaxed when it comes to following rules, which means the youngest child doesn't develop traits of a conformist. They are used to being pampered and showered by attention. Since parents are more lenient with youngest borns, they don't tend to be very rule oriented or revere established authority. There is a tendency to make their own rules, and create new paths rather than walking commonly walked paths.

Typical personality traits revealed by last borns are rebelliousness, empathy, creativity, high sense of self-worth or self-esteem and stubborn. The youngest child often displays traits related to attention-seeking, sociability, extroversion, and manipulativeness. They make for great sales professionals and know how to get their way around people.

A study conducted in 2001 revealed that last-born children show an inclination for careers related to creative arts, and the outdoors. On the contrary, firstborns show an inclination for intellectual vocations.

Only Child

Now, again, the stereotype about an only child being self-centered or creative is not entirely without a strong reason. Since they spend a lot of time in solitary activities, they tend to be creative, entertaining and innovative. They always find resourceful ways to keep themselves busy, earning self-entertainment skills.

Much like first-borns who get used to having their parents' undivided attention until their siblings are born, only children are often self-assured, confident, meticulous and articulate. Since only children don't have to compete with siblings for their parents' attention or material belongings, they tend to develop a sense of self-entitlement and self-centeredness.

They get used to having things their way and find it challenging to cope when things do not happen as they desire. Firstborns always want to be the important people around and have a hard time sharing the limelight with others. Another most marked trait about only child is they are perfectionists. Owing to the fact that their only role models are their parents or other adults in the family, they tend to become huge perfectionists.

Factors That Make the Reading More Accurate

There are many factors influencing an individual's personality that can make your reading more accurate. Psychologists often suggest looking at a person's siblings while analyzing his or her personality since two children within the family rarely share the same role. You will know the role played by the individual you wish to analyze by observing his or her siblings.

Some other factors affecting your reading are genetics and gender. A majority of our personality is determined by gender and genetics in addition to the birth order, which means these are also factors worth considering while analyzing a person's birth order.

Communication Styles of Different Personalities

One of the best and biggest advantages of analyzing people is being able to communicate with them more effectively. It is about forging strong professional connections, building more fulfilling interpersonal relationships and minimizing the scope for conflict.

An individual's inherent communication style is determined by the manner in which he/she interacts with or attempts to interact with others. It is determined in the way they relate to other individuals and how what they say is generally interpreted.

Different personality types are known to communicate in different ways. For instance, in the Briggs Myers personality, ESTJ people may find it easier to communicate within the ST personality group (ESTJ, ESTP, ISTP, ISTJ) than say people from the NF (ENFJ, INFJ, ENFP, INFP) personality group.

Since the Briggs Myers is known to be one of the most comprehensive categorizations of people's personalities, it is valuable to know how each personality type communicates and how to communicate with them to achieve optimal and favorable results. These insights can be used anywhere from interpersonal relationships to professional settings to hobby clubs.

You can determine the personality types of your employees or new hires, or business associates, and use the approach that works best for them while dealing with them for maximizing productivity. The Briggs Myers personality test can be excellent for everything from hiring new employees to analyzing the personality of a potential life partner.

When you know the communication style and preferences of each personality type, it is easier to communicate with them in a more connected and relatable manner.

This is simply because ST people process information and communicate it in a more logical manner than NF people, who are more emotional and intuitive in their communication.

The ST Group

ESTJ

ESTJ people are more open, logical and demanding in their approach to communication. They are essentially deadline oriented and expect things to be completed as discussed and agreed. You won't get too far by involving topics that stimulate an emotional response. Rather appeal to their logical side by offering features/benefits, using more visual aids, offering examples and demonstrating immediate benefits. They often find it hard to express their inner most feelings.

Their people skills aren't much evolved especially when it comes to being patient and gentle with people. The communication style is more open, straightforward and direct, which can hurt other personality types or worse, provoke them.

Stick to practical solutions, data (to back you arguments) and exchange of logical opinions while communicating with the ESTJ type.

ESTP

ESTP type people are dynamic and active communicators and know how to influence, captivate and persuade others through words. Some people can be offended by their direct approach though. Bring variety while communicating with an ESTP personality type. Be more energetic and enthusiastic when you're trying to persuade them.

Like ESTJ, they aren't very comfortable talking about emotions and feelings and like to keep discussions focused on practical, actionable solutions. They address and approach issues with a more rational angle. Be solution-oriented if you want them to get things done or buy your idea. Winning their affection becomes fairly easy when you can put forth logical arguments and practical solutions.

ISTJ

ISTJ type people are natural, straightforward and open communicators. They lay emphasis on precision in their communication pattern. You won't cut it with them by presenting vague arguments and figures. These guys are sticklers for exactness and rules.

They are action oriented and practical in their strategies, which is why most other personalities make a beeline for them when wise, actionable counsel is needed. They find it tough to discuss or talk openly about issues related to love or other emotions. It just may not evoke the desired response from them. Stick to rational discussions, and convince them with precision and accuracy.

Since they are specific, self-assured and logical by nature, they appreciate specifics, confidence, and reasoning. Appeal to logical side by offering well-thought and researched analytic arguments. Demonstrate instant advantages and benefits, while selling ideas, arguments or products to them. Always offer them clear examples and utilize visual aids while explaining concepts.

ISTP

ISTPs are again more direct in their communication and similarly, appreciate a straightforward and open communication approach. They don't take too well to individuals who possess an overly demanding personality.

The ISTP personality type is not very comfortable when it comes to showing tact, empathy or consideration. Some people are invariably affected by their direct and open style of expressing opinions. Again, the ISTP too, struggles with emotional experiences. They find it tough to express their inner feelings.

Don't focus too much on feelings and emotions if you really want to make the communication easy and relatable for them. On a personal front, come up with more practical measures as well as actionable strategies to address their everyday problems.

Professionally, again, exchange more logical arguments or tangible solutions that appeal to their sense of reasoning.

The NT Group

ENTJ

ENTJ highly appreciate manners, order, decorum, and respect. They may appear more demanding when it comes to important issues. They love to swap or exchange views with others, with the fine print that they will go all out to ensure that their opinion alone is right.

Their approach while interacting with people is more business-like, self-assured and objective. It can come across as bossy, but that is the way they communicate. They like confident and business-like communicators who come straight to the point in a professional manner.

They aren't completely at ease when it comes to demonstrating virtues such as tact, patience or emotions. ENTJs are more intense in their professional communication. Ask for their authoritative or expert opinion on any matter if you really want to impress them. Discussion of ideas, practical solutions and analytical opinions related to various subjects may help you win their attention.

INTJ

INTJs are constantly engaged in the pursuit of trying to find out how things are structured, and what changes can be brought about in the structure for good. Their communication pattern and personality essentially involves figuring out the minutest details about things, and them improving it.

They are pleasant and easy conversationalists, without an air of arrogance or formality, but they don't appreciate over familiarity too quickly. Take time in establishing a rapport with them rather than trying to act overtly friendly on the first meeting itself.

The INTJs, pretty much like others in the NT group, struggle with diplomacy and patience in dealing with people. They stick to tradition and established norms even though they may believe it to be a mere formality.

Don't resort too much to emotional topics while interacting with these guys. If they are deducing a concept or argument, make some critical or intelligent comments about the concept to win their admiration.

They appreciate communicating with people who make to the point and well-thought arguments. INTJs are introverts by nature, but they are capable of spreading the enthusiasm and energy when that took in by a particularly exciting idea.

ENTP

They try to seek logical explanations for every phenomena and occurrence and thrive in offering a clear explanation for it. Recognize their elaborate logical inferences if you really want to cut it with them.

ENTPs are interesting and exciting, and easy to converse with. However, owing to a penchant for logical reasoning, the discussions can get adversarial at times. They can be extremely independent and opinionated in their approach, and love to communicate with people of similar intellect.

They are precise, self-assured and confident. They go all out to keep a more objective, analytical and methodical approach towards problems and discussions. This is true even for topics related to feelings and emotions. They will analyze emotions and inner feelings.

They are active communicators and find great pleasure in exchanging opinions, concepts, critical analysis, new approaches, and ideas.

INTP

INTPs have an inherent need to categorize things for authenticating their categorizations.

As communicators, they are respectful, precise, well thought and distant. You won't find an instant warmth or cordial approach when communicating with them. However, they love to engage in logical debates with people of similar intelligence. They don't like superficial conversations, like to keep a tight social circle of like-minded folks.

They like to assess everything objectively, even while debating topics closely linked with feelings and emotions. Thus, emotional subjects don't cut it with them. Communicate with them by making critical comments about their deduced categorizations.

The SF Group

ESFJ

ESFJ people are concrete, responsive, supportive and practical in their interaction with others. They are sure of their logical reasoning and go all out to share it with others. Their communication style is softer but often assertive. They love to converse with diverse groups of people about daily affairs as well as experiences.

Refrain from bringing up very technical discussions or scientific concepts, since they are more focused on immediate, practical, workable solutions. They are great at resolving practical issues (related to management and interpersonal relationships).

ISFJ

They are friendly, thoughtful and supportive communications, who are also pragmatic and to the point. However, they take offense when their assistance or counsel is disregarded. While communicating with them, give them the impression that you appreciate and will work upon their helpful suggestions.

The ISFJ people make a great effort to build consensus for their opinion during conversations. They appreciate minding all rules and manners related to communication, and they are firm in their values.

Logical reasoning and theoretical concepts do not interest them much; hence keep discussions related to scientific concepts and technical topics to their minimum.

They typically don't have a very large social circle, which comprises mainly of people who seek to share their experiences and opinions on issues related to morality, actions, and behavior. They succeed in resolving issues in a practical and actionable manner.

ESFP

These are emotions and feelings people. It brings more meaning into their communication. They are easy communicators and find meaning in feelings. They demonstrate a sense of warmth and trust when discussing with other people. Be sincere and attentive while communicating with them. Their energy and empathy engages people and creates a lively, buzzing atmosphere.

Create a more cheerful, positive and festive atmosphere while communicating with them and you'll make the cut. They exude a deep sense of positivity and are constantly engaged in the pursuit of having open and elevated conversations that lighten the spirit. ESFP folks are more focused on finding easy and fast solutions for practical tasks that are related to building warm and fulfilling relationships.

Be more supportive, self-assured and expressive while communicating with them. Offer examples and highlight immediate advantages, benefits, and profit to help them buy into something.

ISFP

ISFPs are empathy communicators who assume the problems and pains of others as theirs. While communicating, their attention is almost always focused on various emotions. They are always keen on providing emotional support and help to other people while conversing, thus creating a more positive and good-natured interaction channel.

Again, topics that are heavily based on reasoning, logic and theoretical concepts do not make the mark where these folks are concerned. When you're trying to communicate something to them or persuade them into buying an idea, resort to feelings and emotions more than science and logic.

They enjoy sharing their feelings and frequently engage in good conversation to lighten their burden. Just don't broach topics that are too heavy, and involve a lot of technical concepts or rational arguments. They will most likely withdraw or bring the focus back to feelings and emotions in any situation. Keep it related to feelings and experiences, and you'll do well.

The NF Group

ENFJ

The ENFJ folks are blessed with exceptional communication abilities and persuasive skills that can be utilized for convincing others into their view point. They are effortless conversationalists who can quickly manage to earn people's trust. The ENFJS will happily go out of the way to offer solutions and help others.

They often lead in-depth discussions on a variety of topics and are self-assured, supportive and energetic communicators. ENFJs personality types are expressive, demonstrative and vocal about their emotions.

They find it fairly simple to communicate with other personality types on multiple topics. ENFJ people generally have a huge social circle and enjoy making new acquaintances and adding to their contacts list wherever they go.

ENFP

ENTPs often seek to understand the issues faced by others and find meaning in making others happy. This is their perception of the worlds and people around them. People's emotions have a deep impact on their spirit, and they are primary guided by the feelings. ENFPs are in their element when it comes to offering assistance and guidance to others.

Few personality types can match their capability in persuading people and inspiring their trust. They are exceptionally good at understanding, experiencing and feeling other people's feelings. The ENFP communication style is driven by their need for developing and inspiring the capabilities of other people. These guys are easy, pleasant and effortless to communicate with.

They abhor monotony, which is reflected in their communication patterns, where they take on in-depth discussions about a huge variety of subjects. Their communication patterns also are diversified to suit different people, which makes it easy for them to communicate with other personality types. They offer to start stimulating discussions, though they have an inherent dislike for heavily analytical topics.

INFJ

Similar to folks in the other NF group, INFJ people derive great pleasure in helping others even in seemingly impossible situations. It offers their existence more meaning and motivation.

Their communication style is more caring, thoughtful, empathetic and supportive. Communicating with this group becomes fairly easy if you focus more on feelings and emotions. Be pleasant, easy and attentive while communicating with them since their inherent disposition is more easy-going.

However, they can appear more standoffish and reserved in their communication. They take time to collect their emotions, events, and thoughts. The INFJ circle social circle isn't very extensive. It consists of a close-knit group of family, friends, and acquaintances.

Be expressive, utilize visual aids, and appeal to their intuition if you want to communicate effectively with them. Throw them challenges and watch them thrive. Rather than focusing on the current problem, try and bring their attention to the bigger picture.

INFP

An INFPs view of things around them is established by notions of right and wrong, and fair and unfair. They are in their element when they think they are doing the fair and right thing.

Few personality types can match their ability to empathize with people and sense people's concerns. They possess an inherent knack for being able to inspire other people's talents and skills. INFPs are capable of offering emotional support to those around them, and hence should be communicated with on a more feeling based and intuitive level. Relate to their spiritual, intuitive side, and you'll win their trust.

Their social circle comprises a large number of people, and their communication patterns can be intense. People are often interested in soliciting their expert opinion on a variety of subjects. They generally prefer communicating through a mass medium than addressing people individually.

Their communication style involves inner feelings related to the soul and all things spiritual. When the discussion is more esoteric conceptual in nature, they find it easy to have a meaningful conversation.

It's easier for INFPs to connect with people who share a more intuitive or feeling type of mindset. If you want to have common ground with them, focus less on reasoning and more on feelings. Their discussion or communication pattern is focused on a more creative and less theoretical nature.

Chapter 11 Pattern Seeking Secrets - Legs & Feet

After countless years of assessing body language and non-verbal variables for meaning, I have noticed one particular habit that most people will adopt when attempting to analyze others. People will almost always and automatically focus their attention towards the face. This is for good reason as these gestures are some of the most accurate portrayals of thought available to you. As we will see later on, its the subtle movements of the eyes and mouth which give away a person's true intentions so readily.

However, what these people often forget to take into consideration is that the other person is also very much aware of this tendency. They are cognizant of displaying such signals and will be consciously attempting to combat this behavior within themselves. They will be trying to mask it for the most part. As I have mentioned previously, this is easier said than done, but a factor nonetheless.

However it is the lower limbs, the feet and legs which often go unnoticed. This is the reason why you should be paying very close attention to them, all of the time. For hundreds of thousands of years our ancestors were largely only concerned with mastering the art of bipedalism, I.e. mastering the ability to walk and run in an upright position when it came to the legs and feet.

Thankfully this is no longer the case. The world of today has us largely just standing and sitting around, and as a result, we naturally forget about what we are doing with our legs and feet. This is why you need to pay special attention to them. The head and face can be intentionally kept still and devoid of emotion. However, the legs and feet will still move, albeit unconsciously for the most part.

Now of course you will need to take the usual context variables into account when assessing lower limb body language signals. We need to preface this by stating that men and women have tendencies to stand and sit in a different manner from one another which will be in part due to clothing choice, anatomy/physiology and just behavior differences in general.

Men and especially younger men are naturally more inclined to sit in an open stance with knees and legs separated and pointed outwards. This is an overt alpha display as they are exposing the genitals. Women will naturally sit in a more closed position with legs crossed at the knees and pointing to one side. Again, this is in part due to clothing choice if wearing a dress or skirt for instance. But may well be due to cultural influences as much as anything else.

Here are some of the key signals to look out for regarding the lower limbs when attempting to analyze others:

Crossed Vs. Uncrossed

As I have previously mentioned, variances here will differ with regards to gender and also within certain cultures. But for the most part a person sitting with their legs crossed is a show of closed and apprehensive thinking. The person will often be guarding something and you should proceed with some level of caution. It may also infer a degree of disinterest and insecurity.

There are also some subtle differences in the way that people cross their legs. The traditional American leg cross or "figure of 4 leg cross" as it's often phrased, is most common. This is where a person will rest the ankle of one leg on top of the knee of the other, creating a figure of 4 shape with the rest of their body.

This will naturally tend to ensure that the person will lean back which creates the classic professor or therapist seated look you see in movies. I had a post-grad lecturer at Stanford who literally perfected this pose. I would always make a mental note of his posture when I sat appraisal sessions in order to master it myself. But I still haven't quite managed it.

This type of pose will still typically indicate closed thinking and apprehension as their leg is forming a barrier to the body, but it does suggest a slight degree of openness as the crotch is exposed. This is in slight contrast to the European leg cross which is more conventional, with both knees crossed one on top of the other with both legs firmly closed. If a person is exhibiting this sort of crossing, it tends to indicate a guarded mindset.

Conversely a person sitting with their legs open and uncrossed, is more a sign of general openness in attitude. It can even signal confidence and dominance so watch out for how you approach a person in a situation such as this. But like everything I am suggesting here, make sure you are always taking the wider context into consideration.

Implications of Leg Direction/Pointing

The general rule of thumb with any limbs with regards to the direction in which they are pointing, is the same across the board. If somebody is sitting down they will unconsciously point their legs or knees to an area of interest. If you are speaking with them and they are pointing their legs towards you, it's a sign of attentiveness, interest and openness to what you are saying.

This is an especially relevant and reliable indicator of interest when they have just sat down. The longer the person sits in a position they are likely to adjust themselves randomly to get comfortable again. This renders any subsequent analysis much less significant and useful.

Conversely the opposite is true if they are pointing their legs away from you. You may have to alter your interaction style as you may have lost them somewhere along the line. This rule also applies with crossing of the legs, especially if you are sitting alongside the person shoulder-to-shoulder.

I watch out for this all of the time. I can be opening a conversation with a stranger on the street who is initially very coy about what I'm saying. At some point I will build enough rapport to where they will switch their leg position from being crossed at the knees, and pointing away from me, to pointing towards me. These are the changes I suggest as being so important to pick up upon, as they are so simple to spot.

Much like the knees and legs in general, the direction in which the feet are pointed is usually significant. They are almost always pointed towards an area of interest. Once more, it is a subconscious show of attentiveness and openness to what the other person is doing or saying.

People will commonly align their feet to point towards the leader or alpha within a group, or to someone with a high degree of natural gravitas. People are always looking for strong individuals to follow, so watch out for this foot movement during social gatherings or within a large crowd of any kind. This easy form of analysis can tell you an awful lot.

The Gravity of Gestures - Arms & Hands

It's not just the legs and feet which can give strong and suggestive meaning with regards to the way in which they are crossed or direction they are pointed. Many of the general rules here also very much apply to the upper limbs of the hands and arms. Like the legs, arms are a very reliable indicator of mood and intention and are usually somewhat more active as they are under greater conscious control.

This however does indicate that whilst the arms and hands are great non-verbal behavior analysis signals, they can be manipulated and controlled a little more easily compared with the legs. This can sometimes lead to false/positive signals. A person will more commonly realize they are doing something with their hands and arms, compared with the lower limbs, and change this behavior to distract from their true intentions.

In general the arms and hands are a defensive barrier to the body and indicate openness and security when in a neutral position by a person's side . Conversely, apprehension and insecurity are expressed when they are crossed in front of the chest. In fact holding anything in front of the body like a bag or papers for instance will signify this barrier being built.

Again the caveat is always context, these indications are just possibilities and percentages when assessing somebody's thinking, but very well worth taking on board nonetheless. The knack to analyzing others will always be a process of stacking reading skills one on top of another.

So here is a look at the key factors to take into consideration when reading upper limb body language, to give you another layer to work with:

Crossed Vs. Uncrossed

Similar to the legs and feet, crossed arms will usually signify closed and protective behavior. This can be on a scale from general disinterest, and perhaps even boredom, all the way to extreme animosity and hostility. This is especially true if the hands are clenched into fists. You will have to assess the context as always and look for other cues like facial expressions to confirm your assumptions either way. Is the person relaxed and smiling? Or do they have a serious frown on their face?

The other form of crossing is done by holding or clenching the upper arms with the hands whilst the arms are crossed. This is a form of "self-hugging" and can be done with both hands/arms in a more obvious manner or with just the single arm with it being held and clenched by the person's side. This type of behavior is usually a female trait and one they typically exhibit when feeling threatened, or just a general sense of insecurity about a situation.

Conversely open arms in a neutral position either placed in front of the person or down by their sides, will suggest the opposite to the above. It signals that they are not threatened by anything in the immediate environment and even ready to greet and embrace others with a handshake or closer bodily contact. It's the first subtle sign of empathy and openness, so watch out for this when you can.

The final significant signal of an uncrossed arm position to take note of is the hands held behind the back. This is more of a dignitary or military stance and is a clear show of confidence and authority. It indicates that the person is so comfortable with handling themselves and their surroundings that they can afford to position the hands behind them, exposing the torso as they do not fear any attack from the front.

Take note of the people who do this as you will instantly know a lot about their current mindset. Conversely exhibiting this arm position yourself when wanting to appear confident and assured is a intelligent move to make.

So whilst the arms are a very good indicator of feeling and emotion when it comes to analyzing others, the hands specifically are even more so. Similar to aspects of the face, signals given via the hands can be extensive. Hands are extremely expressive and dexterous. This means they can be used in more intricate ways to gesture mood and motive, to a greater extent compared to the larger more cumbersome limbs. But it takes a more trained eye to spot them.

It has been estimated that the hands contain more neural connections to the brain than any other peripheral body part, and for good reason. We use the hands to navigate almost everything in the physical world by touch and can both consciously and unconsciously signal such a wide range of intentions as a result. They are able to give standalone signals with regards to the direction they are pointing or in conjunction with other body parts in the form of holding, clenching, scratching and tapping, just to name a few.

Hands are involved in everything from handshakes when greeting, to waving for goodbyes. Along with the fingers they can make the more obvious expressive signals like the western style "thumbs up" or "OK" sign to indicate contentment or validity of a point being made. They can of course also be used for more crass one and two finger gestures. You can use your imagination here!

However where it really gets interesting with regards to the hands, is where they start to interact with other objects. This might be separate body parts such as a scratch of the nose/ear or fiddling with a cigarette packet or pen. These moments are often known as "leaking signals" as they are indicating a momentary glimpse into what the person is really thinking. Again they might be saying one thing with their words but quite another with their hands.

So here is a breakdown of what the key hand movements and gestures can signal:

Hand Position

When assessing hand posture or position, there is really only two considerations to make when attempting to analyze someone. Two considerations which may allude to the way in which the person is thinking and feeling.

The first of these is when the palms are facing up or open to the rest of the room. This is a signal of submissive behavior generally, it's an appeal to honesty and truthfulness and is thought to stem from the time humans would signal a lack of weaponry or potential harmful object at their disposal. It's a suggestion of innocence or that "I don't know the answer" type of gesture.

This concept also very much applies to the handshake, a fundamental gesture of trust. It is a customary greeting virtually everywhere is the world today, and once again can be traced back to more adversarial type encounters. Ancient Greek texts depicted soldiers shaking hands before battle as early as the 5th century BC.

This behavior can be seen all the way up to the modern Japanese Samurai who not only offered the hand as a gesture of peace, but always with the right hand. This was due to there being no left handed Japanese swordsmen as the energy protecting Ki inscription would always be placed on the right side of the tang by the sword smith, to protect the body from evil spirits when sheathed.

Therefore an offer of the right hand would signal they could not draw the sword from across the body on the left hip. There are a number of other analogies of why it's most customary to shake with the right hand, including that of basic hygiene etc. However the Samurai story is certainly the one I like the most.

If a person offers you their hand with palms facing upwards it's a subtle submissive gesture and one of openness to you. It invites you to place your hand on top of theirs with your palm facing down in a more dominating fashion. However it's actually untrue that you can tell a lot more about someone from their handshake as it's such a common gesture, other than the fact it shows confidence and assurance when done firmly.

It certainly say's more about a person's general thoughts and feelings if they do not offer it. Firmer handshakes can be faked quite easily though, to give the impression of sincerity, so I wouldn't pay so much attention to them other than the fact that you should shake hands firmly at all times yourself. My early business mentor would never speak to anyone he knew without first shaking their hand, looking the person directly in the eye before addressing them by their first and last name. I've never seen anybody get so much out of everyday interactions than this guy.

Alternatively a show of the hands being turned downwards, with the palms hiding from view in a more closed position, signals the opposite. It's more a show of strength, authority and possibly even dominance. Watch out for situations where you are talking to somebody and their hands are firmly and obviously placed downwards in front of them on a table or desk for instance. They will certainly need some work to open up and may indeed by hiding something in addition to just their palms.

Conclusion

Thanks for reading this book. A great deal of our emotions is expressed through our arms and hands. The warm embrace of a touch indicates love while a sharp slap translates to anger. Much of our productivity depends on the accuracy of our arms and hands when completing tasks. The movements of the arms and hands are quite obvious as they are used as a complement to verbal expression. Let's consider a few subliminal signals we receive from analyzing the hands and arms.

As our arms expand, we typically appear larger than our normal demeanor. This could be used as a descriptive means to explain how massive a person or object is, or this could be a subtle sign of instigating aggression or dominance. It also indicates spatial awareness. A person could expand the arms to give the subtle signal that they prefer space. It could be likened to "marking their territory." On the contrary, when the arms expand but curve towards the person, this is reminiscent of a hug. This embrace indicates safety or protection. Many mother figures are seen welcoming their children in this manner.

Since we primarily use our hands and arms to gesture, they are extremely descriptive tools that express our emotions. When the arms are raised, this is a sign of frustration and overwhelming doubt. We can almost envision an overwhelmed person clenching their hands over their ears or on top of the head as a means of protection.

The crossing of the arms is a true indicator of how a person is feeling. As previously mentioned, when the arms are crossed, this typically means anxiety, shyness, fear, or disbelief. We can picture a frustrated mother or father crossing their arms towards their child when they do something naughty. However, when the arms are tightly crossed with the hands either balled into fists or nestled in the armpits, this signals combat. This occurs when an individual has been taunted. Their anger is essentially holding their arms inward as a protective means. The hidden fists could signal the person holding themselves back from doing something they would regret.

Individuals who have been exposed to violence or who feel vulnerable may have a strong dislike for people speaking to them with their hands in their faces. Even a slight gesture could signal a fight or flight response. When the arms are thrusting forward, this is a scare tactic usually intended to create emphasis. We fight with our arms and hands, so the connection between the two is threatening.

When the arms are positioned behind the backs and out of sight of the person they are engaging with, this indicates hidden intent. The person may lack confidence, or they are attempting to hide their fear through fiddling with their hands behind their backs. This isn't necessarily a sign of a liar. Rather, the person may simply feel uncomfortable, or they are preventing themselves from saying something.

The elbows, when facing out, could be a silent cry for space. A person may want others to back away from them without having to actually verbally express their disposition. This can easily be observed through the actions of children. Toddlers, who cannot communicate verbally, will often extend their elbows in a sharp motion in order to indicate space. As adults, we do this subconsciously as a means of inner protection.

The hands are quite detailed in their means of communication. One move of the hand can indicate an invitation while another movement could ignite conflict. When the hands are crossed with the thumbs tucked under, this is a signal of peace. East Indian gurus can be seen holding their hands in this way to express giving, peaceful natures. They wish to extend this light to others through their physical movements. When the hands are placed in front of the belly button, with the fingers touching and open palms, this is a symbol of dignity. The person is trying to show their partner that they are confident, professional, and conscientious.

The hands are also key indicators of direction. We use our fingers to point towards areas of interest. When the hands are placed delicately on the knees with the palms down, this could indicate submission, especially when leaning towards the opposite person. Women usually engage in this stance while attempting to show interest in a flirtatious manner. Hand gestures can also indicate movement. When the palm is facing a person, this translates to dismissal and disapproval. The person is using their hands to physically block the other person from their sight.

When the hands are touching parts of the face, this could translate to brainstorming, boredom, or even decision making. When the palms are essentially holding the face and cheeks upward, this is a clear indicator of a person attempting to wake themselves up from a boring situation. It shows disinterest in the most obvious of ways. However, when the index finger is pointing towards certain areas of the face, a person could be deep in thought. The positioning of the fingers as well as the firmness of their grasp is telling.

Excessive shaking that permeates throughout the palms and into the fingers occurs during high stress situations. A person may be so nervous, their hands begin to shake uncontrollably. This also is a sign of intense hunger. The hands and fingers begin to grow unsteady, thus displaying the body's lack of food. Slight trembles can also occur when a person is being caught in a lie or confronted for a mistake. They may be so angry that the shakes are their way of expressing that anger.

We use our hands to describe the size and stature of certain things. Much like the arms, they are used to accentuate the gravity of a story, describe the weightiness of a subject, and even demonstrate movement. They are our primary way of gesturing, and they can add great excitement to a story or a conversation. When working together with the arms, the hands can be a great indicator of a person's confidence. Touching creates a sense of warmth and community that connects people together. When analyzed carefully, the movement of the hands and arms can tell us key clues about a person's disposition.

Now you know how to read people like a book. Your life will become so much easier now that you have finished this book and learned the critical life skill of reading other people.

You can become a better person by knowing how to read people. Reading people allows you to develop empathy. You can tell what others are feeling and respond accordingly. Your sensitivity will make you a more responsive and caring lover, parent, friend, and family member.

You can also protect yourself better from the harm of people with bad intentions. When you are able to read people, you are consequently able to spot people that will not benefit you. Before you get too far into a relationship of any nature with someone harmful, you can see what the person is about and prevent further harm from happening.

When it comes to choosing a good friend or lover, you are now better able to pick people that are good for your life. You can spot those that actually care for you and have the capability of treating you well. You can pick lovers and friends that have good track records.

All of these benefits are now yours. Thanks for reading.

If this book has been useful to you and you like it, I suggest you also read these my books

"Body language of people"

"Manipulation psychology"

"Persuasion Skills"